Achievement Nudge™

Achievement Nudge™

Softer Than a Shove ★ *Stronger Than a Suggestion*

By Bill Truby
With Joann Truby

Mt. Shasta, California

Achievement Nudge™
By Bill Truby
With Joann Truby

Published by Angel's Dream Publishing Company
P.O. Box 1440
Mt. Shasta, California 96067
Tel; Fax; Pager; (800) 800-8910

www.TrubyAchievements.com
info@trubyachievements.com

Copyright © 2013 by Bill & Joann Truby and Truby Achievements
"Achievement Nudge™" is a Truby Achievements Trademark
Cover design, interior design and illustrations: Bill Truby

Notice of Rights
All rights reserved. No part of this book may be reproduced or transmitted in any form or by any means, electronic, mechanical, photocopying, recording, or otherwise, without the prior written permission of the publisher. For information on getting permission for reprints and excerpts, contact Bill Truby at Truby Achievements.

Notice of Liability
The information in this book is distributed on an "as is" basis without warranty. While every precaution has been taken in the preparation of this book, neither the author, the editor, or Truby Achievements shall have any liability to any person or entity with respect to any loss or damage caused or alleged to be caused directly or indirectly by any information in this book.

ISBN 0-9725897-2-4
Printed and bound in the United States of America by LSI

Dedication

Bill...

I dedicate this book to my Dad who taught me common sense, to put myself in other people's shoes, and that there's always a way.

Joann...

I dedicate this book to my Dad...I'll always remember the lessons and gentle nudges you gave me about how to live my life. I carry your memory in my heart and soul. You are a part of my every thought and action.

> I love you Dad,
> Your Buttercup

*Both of our Dads are gone now...
but their spirit and influence continues to live,
and nudges us on.*

Achievement Nudge™

Softer Than a Shove ★ Stronger Than a Suggestion

Other Books by the Authors

No Two People See the Same Rainbow

The Door

Successful Delegation

Corporate Culture Training Reference Book

Table of Contents

Preface xi

Achievement Nudge #1
Robotic Vacuum Cleaner 17

Achievement Nudge #2
Persistence in Being, Not Doing 21

Achievement Nudge #3
Wisdom from the Berry Bush 25

Achievement Nudge #4
The Bridge of Now 29

Achievement Nudge #5
Phantom Pain 31

Achievement Nudge #6
What are You Worth? 35

Achievement Nudge #7
Make Possibilities Probabilities 39

Achievement Nudge #8
Cow Tipping 43

Achievement Nudge #9
Hedonic Adaptation 47

Achievement Nudge #10
A Party Trick 51

Achievement Nudge #11
Weeds 55

Achievement Nudge #12
Free Will from Free Won't 59

Achievement Nudge #13
   End of History as You Know it 63
Achievement Nudge #14
   Free FROM to be Free TO 67
Achievement Nudge #15
   Don't Ask "Why?" 71
Achievement Nudge #16
   Frying Pans 75
Achievement Nudge #17
   Struggle In Your Mind..79
Achievement Nudge #18
   A Map Isn't the Territory...83
Achievement Nudge #19
   Kissing and Hugging..87
Achievement Nudge #20
   Good News Re: Bad Habits..91
Achievement Nudge #21
   Loss Aversion...95
Achievement Nudge #22
   Sunk Cost Effect 99
Achievement Nudge #23
   Spooky Action at a Distance..103
Achievement Nudge #24
   Rules Give Fun and Freedom 107
Achievement Nudge #25
   Calves and Beauty Queens...113
Achievement Nudge #26
   Can You Lick Your Elbow?...117

Achievement Nudge #27
   The Drip Or the Stream? 121
Achievement Nudge #28
   Driving a BMIR 125
Achievement Nudge #29
   Learn from the Dutch 129
Achievement Nudge #30
   100-Year-Old Man 133
Achievement Nudge #31
   Ants, the Next Super Power 137
Achievement Nudge #32
   Temptations 141
Achievement Nudge #33
   Do You Work? Or Do a Job? 145
Achievement Nudge #34
   Why We Wear Pants 149
Achievement Nudge #35
   When it Matters 153
Achievement Nudge #36
   The Aikido Approach 157
Achievement Nudge #37
   Ten Foot Ceilings 161
Achievement Nudge #38
   Polymodal Sequence System 165
Achievement Nudge #39
   Patience From Perspective 169
Achievement Nudge #40
   Wi-Fi 173

Achievement Nudge #41
    How Happy Are You? 177
Achievement Nudge #42
    Keeping Up With the Joneses 181
Achievement Nudge #43
    Last Words on the Titanic 185
Achievement Nudge #44
    Psychology of Giving 187
Achievement Nudge #45
    Can Money Buy Happiness? 191
Achievement Nudge #46
    The Bat and Ball Problem...195
Achievement Nudge #47
    Expressions of Love...199
Achievement Nudge #48
    Stop Promoting..203
Achievement Nudge #49
    Wink 207
Achievement Nudge #50
    You Can be a Placebo..211
Achievement Nudge #51
    Lost Fingers..215
Achievement Nudge #52
    Dad Doesn't Retire 219

Acknowledgment 221

Preface

I received a large packet of wild flower seeds once and decided to spread them in our "yard." It's not a traditional yard since we live on a few acres in the woods at an elevation of about 4000 feet.

We love our mountain home with its unobstructed view of 14,180 foot Mt. Shasta. The animals and trees provide a peaceful sanctuary, while the views create a great deal of inspiration. Back to the seeds...

I didn't know how well the seeds would "take;" but, with mild interest, I watched where I scattered them and, sure enough, little green plants eventually started to come up. It took them a while due to our elevation.

For quite some time, they didn't look like much. But one day, as if directed with the baton of the "wild flower orchestra master," they all bloomed. And the sight was beautiful.

History of the Achievement Nudge:

That's parallel to the story of what happened with the Achievement Nudges.

Our business has an Achievement Club that anyone can join. When they do, they have access to "mini-training-videos" on all sorts of topics. There is a Business Library and a Personal Library. But we wanted to give our members more.

In the middle of one sleepless night, an idea came to me: "How about inspiring people by sending them something to focus on every week; something to do that would make their life better, happier, more fulfilling."

I figured it would be a "teaching" that would nudge the person to do something differently. And that's where the idea came for the name, "Achievement Nudge."

The first thing I did was to Google the name, "Achievement Nudge." I put quotes around it so Google would search for the exact phrase. It's a good exercise. When you do this, you can see how many other people are using that name, and how many websites are about that concept. If, for example, you Google, "mashed potatoes," you get 4,430,000 results, showing there are that many websites that have that phrase in them.

Do you know how many I got when Googling "Achievement Nudge?" Zero. That's right. Nada. Nothing. Zip.

I was excited. I had come upon a name that was truly unique. No one else in the world was using that name (at least on websites). Of course, I trademarked it.

The Response:

I started sending the Achievement Nudge out every Tuesday morning by email and was amazed at the results. Before long, there were hundreds of people opening their email every Tuesday to read the nudge. People we talked to said, "I can't wait until Tuesday morning to get my coffee and read my nudge!" Some began calling it "Truby Tuesday."

We then began receiving emails about how a certain Nudge would touch someone's life. Nearly every week, ***someone*** would write, *"That was the best Nudge ever!"* Even though everyone seemed to appreciate the Nudges and were helped by them, it also seemed that ***every*** nudge was ***significantly*** important to ***certain*** people. I guess it was where they were in life at the time. A specific Nudge would synchronistically resonate with their situation.

We were very moved. Some would share a certain Nudge's content with a family member or friend, so others were beginning to be helped by this ripple effect. The wild flowers were blooming…and spreading!

Joann and I were overjoyed. This is why we exist - to touch people's lives in a positive way, and this little effort of a weekly Achievement Nudge was doing just that. What a blessing!

The Writing:

Though I write the Achievement Nudge, I couldn't do it without Joann. In fact, she is the inspiration for all I do. I've told her often, "I can move that mountain, if you are by my side."

Joann is my wife and business partner. She has incredible talent and is the most powerful Life/Business Coach I know. She uses these talents to help me with the Achievement Nudges. In addition to sparking an idea for a Nudge now and then, she will also read each one and give me input about it's power, or not...(Yes, some have not made it through to print); what needs to be clarified, what I also need to say, and what I shouldn't say...(Apparently, some of MY content wasn't appropriate for your eyes). She is a valuable and integral part of the Achievement Nudge process.

I'll confess this too: I've always liked to play with words...and use puns. I am convinced that it is a higher form of humor, even though the groans of some of my family and friends would say otherwise. Nevertheless, this weird talent of "connecting the dots" between words that may not be naturally associated is evidence of something that happens naturally for me.

Because of this "sickness," I've had fun linking unrelated ideas with profound lessons in these Achievement Nudges. You will see this in the lesson associated with a Robotic Vacuum Cleaner, or the Dikes the Dutch built. But I can promise you this, EACH lesson in EACH Achievement Nudge is simple, practical, and (based on the experience and feedback of others) will have a powerful affect in your life.

The Content of the Achievement Nudges:

I didn't intend for these Nudges to be exhaustive in how they covered a topic, or for them to be scholarly works with everything perfectly documented. Instead, I wanted to draw from my history with its varied sources of ethics, beliefs, teachings and, more importantly, learnings. My inspiration came from the following places:

- My deeply held spiritual beliefs that give me purpose, meaning, reason and inspiration.

- The common sense that comes from my Cowboy heritage and growing up on a farm.

- My love of the sciences, especially psychology and quantum physics.

- The belief that relationships and the motivation of selfless love combined with unconditional acceptance are key to happiness and fulfillment

- And, above all, my belief (and teaching) to live life freely, on purpose, with purpose. (Freely: Nothing in the past hinders or harms you; On Purpose: Living life using the power of choice; and With Purpose: Having meaning in all you do).

Because of these foundational concepts, you will see themes reappear in the Achievement Nudges:

- Be conscious all the time
- Awareness and ownership of who you are, what you do and what you believe - as compared to letting history shape your "be" and "do"
- The past is gone; learn from it, plan for the future but live in the present - in this way you don't let your past dictate your future

- The core driver of all you feel and do comes from your perspective, your belief about what you are experiencing at the moment - YET, you can choose your beliefs
- The POWER of choice
- The RIGHT to have freedom
- The incredible amount of possibilities and potential we all have
- How the tenacity of decision creates an unstoppable force

These represent some of the underlying, powerful concepts embedded in these Nudges. May they be a companion guide to your life, a resource for your direction, and a power to your purpose.

Achievement Nudge #1

Robotic Vacuum Cleaner

Are you as smart as a robotic vacuum cleaner? A lot of people, and a lot of companies I know…AREN'T!

There are robotic vacuum cleaners you can buy now that are brilliant. No, they can't solve world hunger, nor can they predict where the stock market is going, but they can do THEIR job incredibly well, efficiently and without error. They can even run to the wall and plug themselves in when their battery is getting low. How do they do this? They learn from failure. They never repeat a mistake.

When you place the vacuum cleaner robot on the floor and turn it on, immediately it goes to work. As the cleaner moves around the floor it will invariably run into the leg of a chair, a TV stand, a set of stairs or a wall. Now the fantastic thing is the robot never runs into the same thing twice. It never repeats a mistake. Better efficiency, ease of operation, and greater success come from these "mistake moments." Here's how it works.

When the robot makes a mistake by bumping into something, it LEARNS and doesn't do it again…ever! The vacuum cleaner has a goal, a mission. If anything gets in the way of that mission, the vacuum cleaner learns never to let that happen again. A mistake or a momentary failure becomes a gift that leads to greater success. Human "vacuum cleaners" aren't like that.

I've seen so many individuals, teams, departments, leaders and complete companies continue make the same mistakes over and over again. They'll even complain about repeatedly making the same mistake, often blaming someone else for that mistake.

If the robot behaved like that, it would keep running into the same wall but rationalize it by saying, "It's YOUR fault, YOU put me in this room with walls!" Seems a bit ludicrous, right? But common in people. All too common.

The nudge is simple and clear. When you make a mistake or do something that doesn't give you the result you want, learn from it. Ask yourself, "What caused it?" Get a clear understanding of where the wall is, what caused you to run into it, and what can prevent you from ever running into it again.

Begin by finding the mistakes you repeatedly make, then focus on learning from every little mistake or "turn-around" you make throughout the day. If you learn from your mistakes, false starts, or actions that don't give you the return you were looking for, it will be a great gift toward your success and happiness.

Oh…and don't forget to model that other trick the robot vacuum cleaner performs – the one of running over to the wall to plug itself in when the battery is getting low. Take care of yourself. If YOU don't keep your batteries charged, who will? It's most certain that others won't. They are often the ones who are making the mess you have to vacuum up!

Now back to the sobering question…Are you smarter than a robotic vacuum cleaner? Check out whether or not you keep running into the same wall and the level of your battery. That will tell you.

ACHIEVE GREATER SUCCESS FROM FAILURE MOMENTS

Achievement Nudge

Achievement Nudge #2

Persistence in Being, Not Doing

Is persistence doing something with dogged determination until you achieve your goal? No, it's really not. An insight hit me and I found a weird and wonderful fact. Persistence isn't about doing. It's about being!

A drop of water can wear away a strong boulder, IF it is persistent. A gentle daisy can grow through a thick asphalt road, IF it is persistent. Can you achieve? Yes, IF you are persistent. But you must understand what persistence is.

Is persistence beating your head against a wall until something breaks – hopefully the wall? Is it sticking with something until you reach the goal? Does persistence have to do with gritting your teeth and making it happen? I don't think so. Why do I say that? The reason hit me when I thought about the drop of water and the daisy.

I saw persistence, but I didn't see dogged determination in the drop of water. I didn't see unswerving resolve in the daisy. I didn't even see a goal they were trying to achieve. All I saw was a drop of water and a flower "persistently" being a drop of water and a flower; doing what drops of water do, and doing what flowers do. They were simply following natural laws…and the incredible achievement followed.

That's it.

A huge bright light of insight exploded in my mind. I instantly knew what persistence was. It wasn't about "doing" it was about "being".

I found evidence of my insight by looking at the origin of the word itself. I found that "persist" comes from the Latin "persistere," which means "to ***stand firm permanently***". Other aspects of the definition include: "to ***continue steadfastly in some state***; to last or endure tenaciously; to ***continue existence***."

Do you notice? The word is not about "doing." It is about steadfastly, tenaciously "being." The dripping water was steadfast in "being" a drop of water. The gentle daisy never gave up "being" a daisy.

I realized the "doing" came from the "being". The drop of water did NATURALLY what drops of water do – it dropped and the hard boulder wore away. The daisy did NATURALLY what daisies do – it grew. And the thick, hard asphalt parted. Their incredible achievement came more from steadfastly ***being*** than it did from steadfastly ***doing***.

> ***They focused on the "who" - what followed was the "do."***

(I couldn't resist. Put a beat to that and we've got some rap!)

Now I believe there are two lessons in this insight that led to this nudge. The first lesson is to stop thinking you've got to persistently DO something. Instead, think about persistently BEING someone. Stay true to yourself.

And the second lesson is this: If you try to persist at anything outside of who you are and your purpose for being, no amount of "pseudo-persistence" is going to achieve anything.

I'm defining pseudo-persistence as "steadfastly doing instead of steadfastly being." In other words, for you thick-headed people like me, pseudo-persistence is continuing to beat your head against the wall when it's clear, the only thing that is breaking is your head.

With those two lessons in mind, the nudge is this: Look at everything you are trying to achieve and see if anything is at cross purposes with who you are and what your purpose is. If you find something at cross purposes, eliminate it or bring it into alignment somehow.

Always let your "doing" come from your "being." Don't try to do or be something you're not. It could damage you. Imagine the daisy trying to do what the drip does, dropping its gentle flowery head onto the boulder over and over. It wouldn't take long to have flowery pulp while the boulder is not influenced at all.

And the saddest thing for the daisy? If it were violating the natural laws of **being** a daisy by trying to do what it doesn't do naturally, by persistently dropping on the boulder, over and over, dropping... dropping...dropping, ***trying to be what it isn't*** – the saddest thing about all of that is that the daisy wouldn't be a daisy anymore.

It would be more like a human.

ACHIEVE WHATEVER YOU WANT THROUGH PERSISTENTLY "BEING"

 Achievement Nudge #3

Wisdom from the Berry Bush

Packaging and presentation is everything. From food at a restaurant, to the clothes you wear, to the words you use…the presentation evokes a response. And that response is directly related to a ***person's perspective about the content***, not the content itself. We learn this from the berry bush.

A berry bush depends completely on birds to perpetuate its kind. Though the bush can produce seeds, it is incapable of taking those seeds anywhere else to plant them. Fortunately (like many of us… snicker), the bush is smarter than it looks. It ingeniously enlists the birds to do its bidding. Here's how it works.

The bush grows a bland and boring seed but wraps it in a sweet, carbohydrate "berry-package" to provide a great experience when it is eaten. When everything is ready, the bush turns the berry red, a color birds like. Now the presentation does all the rest. The bush doesn't have to put out a sign, "All You Can Eat Berry Dinner - $2.99." Nope. The "bird-centered" presentation attracts the bird and provides a wonderful experience which ultimately carries out the bush's wishes.

Through natural results of this "bird-centered" experience, the bird performs beyond the bush's expectations. After eating the berry, the bird carries the seeds inside its tummy for a few hours, wraps them in fertilizer and "deposits" them in places the bush can never get to, thus perpetuating the berry bush species.

And the bird does even more. Not only does the bird want to have repeat "berry eating" experiences, it flies around advertising for the bush by speaking of that experience – "Cheep, Cheep, CHEAP, CHEAP."

Huge marketing studies and curious scientists have proven what the bush already knows – packaging and presentation is everything. We humans respond just like birds. Even we won't like the berry if it isn't packaged well, if the color, shape or smell is off in some way.

This packaging principle is true in all aspects of life. A pile of food at a restaurant will have a totally different experience…and taste… than if the same food is presented beautifully. The packaging of "you" creates an experience for another person. Your clothes, words, attitude, and personal power (or lack thereof) all present a package and presentation that makes you attractive…or not.

Intuitively, we know this. We dress up for a job interview. A candlelight dinner doesn't literally make the food taste better. It just feels like it tastes better because of the *experience* of the presentation - how it all looks and feels.

The trick is to create a better package and presentation for all of the things that matter. It's really better for both people involved. As an employer, a friend, a spouse, a parent – if you want someone to perform a certain action or believe a certain truth, package and present it in a way that is attractive to the other person. Prepare it right, and the person's actions will be just as natural and automatic as the bird and the berry. Mess up the package or presentation and it will give the "bird" a bad experience, causing it to leave with a bad taste in its mouth. When that happens, the bird doesn't want a repeat experience.

Now…I'm happy that we humans have evolved a bit and use this packaging principle in a more civilized way. When *WE* package and present our request to someone, we can expect that person to carry out our business using their head. Unlike the bush, we don't have to wait for some "bird-brain" to carry out our bidding…well…from the other end.

ACHIEVE BETTER RESULTS FROM OTHERS BY A BETTER PACKAGING AND PRESENTATION OF YOUR REQUESTS AND DESIRES

Achievement Nudge

Achievement Nudge #4

The Bridge of Now

A bridge makes it easier to get across places that would otherwise slow you down or stop you. It's true on land. And it's true in life.

Bridges have been around since humans existed. A fallen log drug into place made it easier to get across a stream or even a large chasm. When the Romans invented the arch, bridges took a huge leap in their ability to span wider and wider expanses.

A simple but consistent fact about a bridge is this: A bridge is not a stopping place. A bridge is used on your journey as you focus beyond the chasm you are crossing.

In life, a bridge can be anything from a friend in need, to medication. It can be a loan until you get your new job, or a "fixer upper" cottage while you wait to afford your dream home. A degree in college can be a bridge to a new career, as can a rental car be a bridge to get you around until your damaged car is repaired. All of these are bridges to something better. They are not stopping places.

A time period can be a bridge too; a bridge on your journey from here to there. This nudge is to think about *the time period you are in now.*

Achievement Nudge

Think of *NOW* as a bridge.

Now, let's look at a few "bridge rules" you need to follow as you walk the "*Bridge of Now*."

1. First, you can't get to the other side unless you let go of this side. Let go to move on.

2. Second, make sure you're on the bridge that leads you to where you want to go. It would be disappointing to get to the other side and find you're going the wrong way.

3. Third, depending on how precarious your bridge is, don't look down. You'll get to the other side just fine if you watch where you're going.

Achieve consistent and positive momentum on your life-journey by choosing and using bridges

 Achievement Nudge #5

Phantom Pain

I hope you're not experiencing phantom pain. But if you are, here's what you can do about it.

My mother-in-law lost the lower part of her right leg because of constricted circulation that came from huge surgery complications. Now she gets along nicely with a prosthetic leg but sometimes experiences a strange effect called "phantom pain."

Phantom pain is common in amputees. It's when you feel pain, real pain, in a limb that is no longer there. Mom felt it in her "foot" that wasn't there anymore. She told me that the pain was the same pain she felt when she still had her foot, and in the same location as if her foot was still there. She said it hurt just as bad too.

Phantom pain is weird. It's weird because it feels absolutely real, coming from a limb that is no longer there. So, what's really going on is a condition of remembered pain. Pain that literally feels real, but it's not currently real.

That's weird, right? Mom feeling pain in a foot that is no longer there, because her subconscious mind remembers the pain she used to have! Yes! That is weird. But hold on, there's MORE weirdness "afoot!" The weirdness of phantom pain is surpassed by the weirdness of its cure, a cure called mirror therapy."

Mirror therapy is simply holding a mirror in front of where the limb used to be, looking at it, and acknowledging that the limb is gone. When you do mirror therapy, the pain goes away...***instantly!***

I applied this therapy to the pain in mom's absent foot and got amazing results. The pain went away immediately, and didn't come back. She thought it was magic.

For me, the weirdest part of this weird pain, and weirder cure, was using the mirror. Why couldn't mom just look at the missing foot and get the same results? Why did she need a mirror? Then I realized this: The power wasn't in the mirror. The mirror was used to manage the mind. Here's how it worked.

A mirror is a dispassionate, objective reflector of reality. If mom looked at the place where her foot used to be, a part of her mind believed it was still there. She couldn't look at the mirror without that part of her mind engaged.

However, we have learned to trust that the reflection in a mirror is real. Holding the mirror in front of her missing foot allowed another part of her mind to believe in the reflection and say, "Your foot is NOT there." And if the foot is gone, there can't be any pain. "POOF." No pain.

How about the pain you feel in life, not your limbs, but your life?

If you're like most people, the perspectives and pain in your life come from your past. And for most people, it is an illusion, a set of feelings that result from the *memory* of things that are no longer there. If this is true for you, you need mirror therapy.

An objective friend, a counselor, maybe a collection of friends; each or all can be your mirror. Ask them to objectively reflect what they see. Ask them, "Do you think there's really something to this? Is my 'foot' really there?" And if your "mirror" says there's really nothing there, and you trust the mirror's reflection, acknowledging its truth, your pain can go away - instantly.

When perspectives and belief change, the reality of what you experience and feel changes right along with it. And it does so instantly!

Now be careful if you try this therapy. Treat the mirror gently no matter what it reflects. Don't attack the mirror because of its reflection. Mirrors are fragile, and "people-mirrors" are even more fragile than glass ones.

Plus, when you break a glass mirror, I hear you get seven years of bad luck. Break a people-mirror, and you just might have a lifetime of bad consequences.

Achievement Nudge

ACHIEVE FREEDOM FROM PAIN THAT ISN'T THERE BY USING A "MIRROR"

Achievement Nudge #6

What are You Worth?

What are you worth? It matters because; your self-worth determines how you treat "you"…as well as how you treat others.

How are YOU valued? If you were sold for parts, such as bone marrow, DNA, lungs, kidneys, heart, etc., you would be worth about $45 million dollars. But if you were sold for the chemicals in your body, you would be worth about $160.00. If you said, "Hey, I'm worth $45 million dollars!" Someone else could just as easily say, "Nope, you are only worth the value of 45 Café Mochas!" It all depends on what valuation criteria you choose.

There are many ways to value ourselves. Some choose feelings as the criterion. They FEEL like a million bucks one day, then FEEL like a failure the next. Many base their worth on what they do… (actually, more on how they think OTHERS value what they do).

But, again, the valuation criterion is what matters. "How much value" is clearly tied to how you DECIDE the "how much."

This is true in all valuations. A piece of paper in our pocket or purse has a number on it. We collectively agreed on a valuation standard, and gave that paper a value. We call it "money." But the value is clearly not in the piece of paper. Try to buy a car by writing a number on a piece of stationary. The laughter will be amusing until the car dealer thinks you're serious. Then he'll probably look scared.

It's the CHOSEN valuation criterion that determines value. And it's the same in valuing YOU. The question isn't, "HOW MUCH are you worth?" It's HOW you determine how much you are worth.

Now, be careful. Certain valuation criteria can also limit value. You can see this problem in all of the criteria standards I mentioned above. Each has a cap. You only have so many organs. You only have a limited amount of chemicals in your body. Your feelings are limited by the ONE at the moment. And you can only DO so much.

So which criterion do you choose, then? How about one that is better than all the rest…AND has no cap.

I'll illustrate it with some history. Around 1700 BC the Phoenicians discovered a way to make purple dye. They carefully extracted a few drops of fluid from the murex, a shell-fish found in the waters off of Tyre and Sidon.

The process was difficult, expensive and rare. It took nearly 60,000 shell-fish to make one pound of purple dye, and you couldn't get it anywhere else in the world. Only the rich could buy purple fabric. And that's why purple came to be associated with royalty. Kings could afford it. Not many others could. The purple dye was valuable because of its rarity. It was one-of-a-kind. The criteria, then? Because it uniquely existed, it was valuable.

Now, back to valuing you…How many "YOU's" are there? Right! Just one. You are unique, AND you exist. Since this is true, you must be incredibly valuable!

And you are. Valuable because you exist. And THAT is the valuation criterion to use. ***Existence!***

You may already know this, but this is the criterion Divine Entities use to value you. It's also the criterion your dog uses to value you. Let it be the criterion YOU choose to value you!

Acknowledge it: You are the only, most important, most valuable person in the world in your shoes. Now, start treating yourself that way!

ACHIEVE GREATER SELF-WORTH BY CHOOSING THE RIGHT CRITERIA FOR VALUATION

Achievement Nudge

# Achievement Nudge #7

Make Possibilities Probabilities

If you think you are stuck in life or don't have any (or many) possibilities for change, think about this…

As you stand on the vista of this next phase in your life, there are countless possibilities for you…if you know they are there. Often, people don't achieve ANY possibilities because they don't see them, let alone know how to pursue them. They may even be discouraged by the odds of success. Years ago, I learned some lessons from the Rubik's Cube that may help.

There are over 43 quintillion different configurations for the Rubik's Cube. That's 43,252,003,274,489,856,000 possibilities to be exact. A simple but true fact was this: before I had a Rubik's Cube I had NONE of those possibilities. None!

It's a simple "duh" but if you don't acknowledge there ARE possibilities, you can't achieve even one. The first part of this nudge is to claim the possibilities that are in your future. Own the reality of countless (and I mean COUNTLESS) possibilities that exist within it. They are all open to you. BUY THE "RUBIK'S CUBE" – (I'm talking about owning the "possibility" for those of you slow to symbolism).

Achievement Nudge

After you own the possibilities, choose one to pursue, then believe it can be achieved…even though the odds seem overwhelming. The Rubik's Cube has 43 quintillion possibilities with ONE as the solution. The odds of success were 53 quintillion to 1. If I tried all of those possibilities on my own it would take more than 13 million years to solve the puzzle. I knew I didn't have that long. I had to make the odds of success better by turning the possibility into a probability. I did that by doing two things: looking at the evidence of achievement, then getting the guidance needed for me to achieve it. How did I do those two things?

I turned the possibility into a probability by asking the question "Is this possible for someone like me?" Ask the same question about what you want to achieve. If the answer is, "Yes," then it's possible for you. And if it's possible, it can become probable. YOU can achieve it too. The inventor of the Rubik's Cube solved the puzzle. If he or someone else couldn't, it wouldn't be possible for you and me. But he did! Now the solution becomes a probable possibility!

Now, get the guidance to achieve it. A book, a friend, a counselor, a teacher…someone who has pursued your possibility before can give you guidance. There's always a scout, an explorer, someone who "has gone where no man has gone before." That person shows us the way. One person solved the Rubik's Cube. Now all of us can.

Believe that possibilities exist in your future. Choose one (or more). Get some guidance. Then go for IT, the "It" you choose. Then, when someone asks you, "How's IT going?" you can give them a knowing smile and say, "Impossibilities have become possibilities because now they exist. I even turned a few of them into probabilities; got the guidance to achieve them, and now 'IT' is going fine!" They'll probably scratch their head and give you a polite smile as they walk away. You'll smile too. YOU know what you're talking about!

Achieve possibilities by making them probabilities

Achievement Nudge

Achievement Nudge #8

Cow Tipping

Don't believe everything you hear. Even more importantly, don't get sucked into wasting energy on things that just aren't valid or true!

Have you heard of "cow tipping?" It is the supposed practice of a person sneaking up on an unsuspecting, sleeping cow…and tipping it over. But, here's the truth: Cow tipping isn't possible.

People have conducted studies, taking the time and energy to calculate the physics of it. And the calculations prove that it would take up to five people to tip a cow, depending on its size. One person just isn't going to do it. The mass of a cow is simply a lot more than one human can handle.

But you don't have to spend the time and energy it takes to calculate the improbability of tipping a cow. There is an easier way. Look at the premise.

Cows don't sleep standing up! Hellllooooo……. *(A modern way of saying a word from the 80's – "Duh!!")*.

Having been raised on a cattle farm, I know this to be true. I saw it. The stereotypical, contented cow lies down, slightly on its left or right side; eyes closed, chewing its cud, peacefully sleeping in a pasture of grass. And a cow lying down is not going to be tipped. Cow tipping is a myth. Simple. Conclusive. Done!

The first Law of Achievement is the Law of Perspective: "Belief determines attitude and action."

It follows: A valid belief or perspective leads to a positive attitude and behavior. But a faulty premise leads to wasted time and energy. And when we are victim of a faulty premise, we don't notice our wasted energy until it's…well…wasted!

I've seen entrepreneurs spend a huge amount of resources to build a business, only to fail because of a faulty belief. They had a whim of what they THOUGHT people would buy. But they didn't conduct preliminary market research to tell them the truth. I've seen energy wasted on training, when discipline was needed. I've seen energy wasted on discipline, when training was needed.

A faulty premise, a misguided perspective, an invalid belief…all can make you unproductive, lessen your profitability, and weaken your leadership. It will waste your time and drain your energy.

Instead, train yourself to start at the nucleus of anything you consider: What is the truth about this? What are the givens? What is real? What is valid? Is this even possible? Always start by validating the premise.

That's your nudge.

Oh…and by the way…we farm kids had a lot more enriching activities we engaged in than that foolish legend of cow tipping. Remind me to tell you sometime about challenging my cousins to climb the manure pile to see who could get the highest.

ACHIEVE MORE BY NOT GETTING SUCKED INTO A FAULTY PREMISE

Achievement Nudge

Achievement Nudge #9

Hedonic Adaptation

We all want to feel good, to experience pleasure. But our minds have the ability to deceive and skew what we think IS pleasurable by a process known as "Hedonic Adaptation."

"Hedonic" has to do with wanting or experiencing pleasure. "Adaptation" has to do with, well…adaptation. Now that we've cleared that up, let's understand how it works.

In the early 70's a number or researchers found that people who were stripped of things that would normally give them pleasure, prison inmates for example, were able to adapt rather quickly to their simplistic lifestyle. Their contentment and pleasure stabilized as they accepted their meager surroundings. This stabilization of pleasure became known as "hedonic adaptation" and it happened quite quickly.

Here is how hedonic adaptation works. We want pleasure. If our ability to obtain new things is limited, we find pleasure in what we have, not what we can get. Our pleasure calibration changes to fit our circumstances.

But hedonic adaptation works against us if the situation goes the other way. When we ADD new things, the pleasure calibration rises to enjoy the new car, promotion, house, jacket – or whatever; but it doesn't last very long. Our hedonistic enjoyment adapts to the new "thing," but then, that new "thing" becomes "normal" driving us to want MORE of it to create pleasure.

Hedonic adaptation works FOR us when things are reduced because we calibrate by what we HAVE. It works against us when we obtain new things because we calibrate by what we can GET!

Addictions can be fueled by hedonic adaptation by wanting more and more of the pleasure substance. Employees who have received a raise can soon want another raise because of hedonic adaptation. The "high" from a new relationship can go away because of hedonic adaptation. And that new dress that makes you look thin and gorgeous can get lost in the closet because of hedonic adaptation. Researchers called this a "hedonic treadmill" – wanting more and more things to find the pleasure we crave.

If you are on a hedonic treadmill, what can you do? Two things help. First, you can try a "reduction." Decide what area of life the hedonic treadmill governs, then choose to simplify it. Step off the treadmill, be in control, and strip away a few things. You will notice how getting rid of some things not only gives you a sense of personal power, but a sense of pleasure. Have you ever cleaned out your closet or desk? That feeling you got? That's what I'm talking about. Hedonic adaptation at work.

Secondly, researchers found that hedonic adaptation tends to have less effect on new ***EXPERIENCES*** than it does when getting new ***THINGS***. This may be because of a time factor. Putting on a new jacket is like taking a gulp of pleasure. Driving to a lake shore with friends for an evening picnic around a bonfire, is like leisurely sipping a soothing cup of tea. Your "hedonistic-meter" doesn't calibrate so quickly with experiences so the pleasure you derive from them lasts longer – much longer.

Without you taking the wheel, hedonic adaptation will be setting the rules and driving you to get more and more things. Instead, YOU take the wheel. Drive by the Goodwill store to strip away what you really don't need or want; then drive to a place where you can experience a sunset. You'll have more pleasure with that experience for a longer time than if you drive to the mall to get some-THING new.

ACHIEVE GREATER HAPPINESS WITH EXPERIENCES RATHER THAN THINGS

Achievement Nudge

Achievement Nudge #10

A Party Trick

Here's a party trick that shows how things are connected. Beware. You can only use this once. It takes a bit of a surprise to pull it off.

Tell people you have a new "Simon Says" game. Have your friends stand to your left in a tight line, shoulder to shoulder; the more people the better.

Now start the "Simon Says" instructions: (Picture this in your mind...)

1. "Simon says, put your left arm straight out in front of you and make the thumbs up sign."

2. "Simon says, kneel down on your left knee (only one knee)."

3. "Simon says, turn your head to the left and look at the back of your neighbor's head."

Your friends have everything on their left side engaged now so they can't readily support or catch themselves. They are on their left knee, their left arm is in front of them, they are looking left so can't see something coming from their right…they are in a precarious position, and don't know it, AND they are all connected in one system.

Achievement Nudge

Now…the fun begins. Make a little nudge to the first person on your left and watch the entire line gently go down like dominoes. Laughter increases while trust in you diminishes.

This little party game illustrates how doing one small act, a positive *or* negative act, has a domino effect, an effect on every element in the system.

Another familiar example of how connectedness works is when you raise the temperature setting on the thermostat of your heating system.

In very simple terms, when you want it warmer in your room, this is what happens: (1) you choose a temperature setting on the thermostat; (2) the thermostat compares the room temperature with your choice; (3) the heating appliance is turned on; (4) the system is turned off when the room temperature matches your chosen temperature.

If ANY of those steps are eliminated or changed in any way, you don't get warm. If the thermostat doesn't work, you don't get warm. If the heating appliance doesn't turn on, you don't get warm. If the fan doesn't come on, you don't get warm. If anything, even a small little wire doesn't connect, you don't get warm. If **_ANYTHING_** changes, the **_ENTIRE_** system changes – **_COMPLETELY_**!

Now you can use this principle in your life. If you change anything in a system on purpose, the outcome changes. It follows, then, if you don't like the outcome you are getting, change the system, and you'll change the outcome. You can even eliminate it entirely with a small act, a small change.

Here's how you can do this. First, take a look at the outcomes in your life that you don't want: Getting angry at your neighbor; a certain employee frustrating you; your not being on time to meetings or finishing tasks; overeating; not having enough time to exercise;…we all have *many* outcomes we don't want in our lives.

Now, change *anything* in the system, and you immediately change the *entire* system, including it's unwanted results. Changing something toward the beginning of a system's flow is often the best - and easiest. Here are a couple of examples.

The next time you get an outcome that you don't like or want, replay the movie of what led up to that outcome. See the "mental movie" in as much detail as possible. What happened first? What were your initial thoughts? What was the feeling you had at that moment? What did you do first? What happened second? Third? Fourth?...

Let's say that you repeatedly get angry at your neighbor, and you find that your initial thought was, "That blanket blank neighbor…", try changing it to, "I wonder what would cause my neighbor to do that?" Change that element and you'll get a different outcome.

If you procrastinate, and your analysis of the flow of thought and action (the system) that leads to procrastination shows that your first behavior was to turn on the TV to have background news, try doing something else instead. Change that one part and the ***entire* system *with it's typical outcomes*** changes.

It's powerful, simple, and sort of obvious when you think about it. You can get a different outcome by simply doing something differently. Common sense, right?

When I was a kid, I heard how "throwing a monkey wrench into the system can shut down an entire factory." I never knew you could do that in real life…and do it on purpose…for good, AND for good!

ACHIEVE BETTER OUTCOMES BY CHANGING ANY PART OF THE SYSTEM THAT LEADS TO THE OUTCOME

Achievement Nudge #11

Weeds

We've all heard it, "We reap what we sow," right? But have you ever thought about having to reap what other people sow? It happens to all of us!

From Scripture to ancient philosophy, there is a truth that we all have heard and experienced. It can be taught to us in a loving tone to help us prepare for our future, or it can be spoken in a harsh tone with a wagging finger from a person reprimanding us about our past. In either case, it's still true. "You reap what you sow!"

But somewhere along the way I found that, though I was growing "plants" that I had sown, there were plants growing in my life-garden that **OTHER** people had sown.

I also was shocked when I realized that I was tending to those plants as if they were mine. I didn't make a distinction between what I had planted and what other people did. When I saw this, I also became aware of the stress, and time, and energy, and resources it took to take care of THESE plants that came from the seeds of other people's plantings.

I would tend these "other's-sown-plants" as if they were mine. I took responsibility for them. Sometimes I even felt as if I caused them. To make matters worse, I realized that these "other's-sown plants" were taking the water and nutrients that MY "self-sown-plants" needed.

Then it hit me. In one profound, life-changing insight, it hit me. Wait a minute…these are WEEDS!!!! Anything growing in my garden that I didn't plant is a WEED!!!

And what do you do with weeds? You "weed" them – you get rid of them. You pull them out of your garden. You don't let them rob the plants you WANT from the limited resources available for growth and an abundant harvest. Whew…what an insight!

How about you and your garden? I nudge you to look around today. In the gardens of your personal AND professional life, see if you are tending to things you didn't plant there. If you are, you are tending to a weed. You are watering a weed. You are feeding a weed. You are ***PERPETUATING*** a weed.

In business, if you're a supervisor, tasks can cleverly get delegated UP. You end up doing things that aren't really your responsibility – a WEED!

In relationships, responsibility for someone else's happiness or well-being can get placed on your shoulders – a WEED!

I have a hunch that if you just took one look today, you'd be able to weed out three things you didn't plant in your life-garden. Keep weeding, and over time, your garden is going to look better, produce more and give you much more happiness.

Wow…I just had a mental movie come to me as I pictured you "getting this" and starting to weed.

I saw some of you getting down on your hands and knees, gently pulling out the weeds so as to not harm the plants you DID plant in your garden.

I saw others excitedly getting out their weed whacker and getting rid of entire sections of weeds.

Then I saw others getting out their chain saws and attacking their garden like a maniac in a horror movie, in a rage, cutting down just about everything in sight! If this is you, BE CAREFUL!! You might throw the baby out with the bath water. Oops, that's the metaphor for the subject of another Nudge.

ACHIEVE THE SAVING OF TIME AND ENERGY BY WEEDING WHAT YOU DIDN'T PLANT

Achievement Nudge

Free Will from Free Won't

It's easier for your subconscious mind to say "Yes." But true learning and growth must often come from saying "No."

Scientific research consistently shows that our subconscious mind controls at least 95% of our day. We are on autopilot more than we know or care to admit. Our subconscious mind is making default decisions for us most all the time; decisions about how to act, what we want, and how we feel. But where does the subconscious mind get the criteria for its choices?

The only criteria our subconscious mind has for making choices is past learning. If a hot stove burns our fingers, we don't have to think about it the next time we approach a stove. Our subconscious is already programmed to make us cautious. Tying our shoes, brushing our teeth, even driving a car; all are more efficiently done by our subconscious mind governing the process.

But our subconscious mind can receive faulty learning or information too. A mother telling us we don't look good in red can be accepted by our subconscious mind as "truth" and make us avoid red clothes when shopping. And faulty information gets perpetuated too.

Now, here's something disturbing. Most of the input our subconscious gathers for making its automated decisions is obtained before we reach 6 years of age. We're talking about all input - positive, negative, faulty, skewed - ***ALL*** input. And the sad, somewhat scary truth about this is: at this early age, we don't get a chance to choose whether the input is valid or not. We simply accept it and perpetuate it.

So today, when presented with the implied question, "Hey, subconscious mind…shall we do what we've always done; believe what we've always believed; feel the way we've always felt?" The answer is a decided "Yes". Our subconscious simply makes a decision driven by pre-determined preferences. Ancestors, parents, culture, society, friends, and every experience we've ever had, all have filled our subconscious mind with data that directs our reaction and choice.

> ***Our subconscious mind is not a logical "evaluator"***
>
> ***It is an emotional "perpetuator"***

Scientists say we don't really have "free will" because of the power of this dynamic in our subconscious mind. But we do have what some authors and scientists call "free won't" – the ability to say "No" to our subconscious inertia.

The subconscious will rule the conscious UNLESS we choose to not let it. Yet, at any time we can turn off the autopilot.

This nudge is to stop and observe. Take into account what your subconscious mind is choosing. That awareness will give you a second choice, the choice to say "No," - NO to a subconscious choice that perpetuates a bad habit or faulty information. Practice saying, "No, I will choose something different, better, healthier – saner." When you do, it gives you greater freedom, more choices, and growth from your pre-programmed, subconscious inertia.

Interesting, isn't it? It seems that "free won't" is the only way to have "free will."

ACHIEVE GREATER GROWTH AND FREEDOM BY LEARNING TO SAY "NO" TO YOUR SUBCONSCIOUS

Achievement Nudge

Achievement Nudge #13

End of History as You Know it

Research shows that your mind thinks you are at the end of your history, the end of the world as you know it. But you're wrong. It's really not true.

In the journal, *Science*, various scientists reported on a research study that shows we think differently of ourselves in the past than we do in the future. They proved that we all acknowledge rather significant changes in our lives over the past 10 years, but we predict little or no change for our future. They called it the "End of History Illusion."

One study involved 19,000 people ranging in age from 18 to 68. In all cases, the person remembered their past self as being quite different than their present self, but saw little or no change in their future. When it came to personalities, tastes, likes and dislikes, the research subjects acknowledged significant differences in who they were ten years ago. But they predicted little or no change ten years from now.

The research also showed that we are all alike. Nothing seemed to have an affect on this mental perspective. Age didn't matter. Nor did the amount of change that occurred over the past 10 years matter. Each person was at the "End of their History" – or so they thought.

Achievement Nudge

Even if we want our future situation to be better (more money, a better job, or to buy our dream home…) when it comes to our "person," our subconscious mind believes we are "there." In the future, we believe we will like the same music, watch the same kind of TV shows, eat the same kind of food, and have the same taste in the clothes we wear now.

To the possible disappointment of those around you (smile), we believe we will be the same person. But the reality is we WILL change. It is inevitable.

Now…normally we spend a lot of energy doing something if we truly believe history is going to end. We have seen that happen in the past, the most recent example (at the time of this writing) surrounds the end of history prediction from the Mayan calendar.

Some people spent hundreds of thousands of dollars to warn the world. Others invested a lot of energy preparing for it. I saw many people travel from around the world to be here in Mt. Shasta where we live. They said they wanted to catch a ride on the space ship they believed would settle on the mountain to pick up passengers and leave this world behind. Still others used a lot of energy criticizing or making fun of the proposed end of the world.

When you believe something is going to happen, you automatically put energy toward dealing with it one way or another. But, curiously, the researchers found that even though we have this "end of history illusion," we don't put any energy into changing it. We just let time take it's course.

So this nudge is to suggest you deal with this illusion in a proactive way. The illusion has our subconscious mind believing there will be no change in us, yet the reality is ***there will be!*** Change WILL happen.

If you are not driving that change, you become subject to outside forces that are. And that describes a victim.

Since change in the future is inevitable, let's be in control of that change. From time to time, assess who and how you are now. Monitor your choices, your decisions. Think about how your choices are changing YOU. Is it for the better or the worse?

You might even want to analyze your past ten years of change to make better choices for your next ten years. Ask yourself, "How am I different? What caused that difference? Was I in control of choosing that difference? Is the difference beneficial? Is there something I want to change for my future?"

You do this and you'll create a new future for yourself. The Mayans were wrong and so is the illusion in your brain. Your future is going to change you. You might as well be in control of it.

ACHIEVE POSITIVE CHANGE BY CREATING A CHOSEN FUTURE

Achievement Nudge

Achievement Nudge #14

Free FROM to be Free TO

Sometimes, freedom to do something differently, to be someone different, to go in a different direction - just isn't enough to be truly free.

I was jogging in a new neighborhood once when a rather mean looking dog began running toward me at full speed. His snarling, barking, aggressive attack came to an abrupt end when he got to the end of his chain. That chain was connected to a sturdy collar and jerked the dog off his feet, leaving him whimpering and helpless on the ground.

Have you ever felt that way? You start excitedly moving toward something you want, full speed ahead. You're going toward what you want to do differently, how you want to be different. The next thing you know you're yanked off your feet, helpless and whimpering on the ground. What causes this? It's because of this simple truth:

Freedom TO do, or be, something different can only come when you're free FROM what prevents you.

"Freedom TO…" only comes after "Freedom FROM…"! I've seen it hundreds of times. From losing weight to developing a healthy self-esteem to achieving a new goal; if a negative behavior is serving you in some positive way, you are chained to it and won't be free to have anything different.

If your subconscious mind believes your hefty body is chained to your identity, your conscious mind won't be free to lose weight. If your poor self-esteem is chained to strong beliefs others gave you when you were young, you won't be free to believe positive affirmations your conscious mind tries to repeat. If your desire to achieve is chained to a fear of success, that chain will yank you off your feet with your subconscious mind screaming, "You will NOT amount to anything!"

If there's ever something you are trying to achieve differently – a new belief, a new behavior, a new way of being – and you can't achieve it, don't sit at the end of your chain whimpering and helpless. Instead, get rid of the chain that prevents the freedom.

You may be able to do this yourself or you might need to find someone with chain cutters. But whatever you need to do to eliminate the chain, do it! I know you can. I've never seen a chain so strong that it couldn't be broken.

When you free yourself FROM what you are chained to, you'll be free TO achieve what you want. At the end of your chain is the end of your possibilities, the end of life as you know it. But there's a whole world of possibilities beyond the chain that is immediately and easily available when the chain is cut.

You will shake your head in astonishment when you find that freedom to roam the entire forest is automatic and instant when you're not chained to that one "blankity-blank" tree anymore!!!

ACHIEVE A "FREE-ER" FREEDOM BY ELIMINATING CHAINS

Achievement Nudge

Achievement Nudge #15

Don't Ask "Why?"

Want to know what happened? Then, don't ask why.

"Why," you ask? I'll tell you – but just this once.

If you want to know the truth about why something happened, don't use the word "why" to find out. If you do, it triggers the other person's brain to answer in a way that clouds the truth. I'll explain the psychology of that.

Most of the time in your past, when you heard the question "Why?" it triggered mixed emotions and, therefore, mixed answers in your brain. At some level, you knew that the person asking "Why?" didn't really want the answer. Instead, it was a veiled attempt to attack YOU. The tone gave it away…

"Why didn't you clean your room, Johnny?" asks an angry parent. But they really didn't want to know "why" – they just wanted to discipline or say, "Clean your room NOW, Johnny!"

A teacher might ask, "Why didn't you get your homework done?" when they were more interested in having you DO your homework than wanting to understand the reason why you didn't get it done.

Achievement Nudge

Even a boss might ask, "Why wasn't that report done on time?" when what the boss really wanted was the report, not the reason for it being late.

Throughout time, we also learned what didn't work. We learned that actually answering the question often didn't help our situation.

An honest answer to our parent, "I was playing with my toys so I didn't clean my room," usually got us into more trouble. Or the parent would say, "Don't get smart with me!" causing more confusion. "My dog ate the homework," answers the question but would likely fuel the teacher's anger. "You didn't give me enough time to get the report done," counterattacks the boss, but doesn't do us any good. We subtly learned that answering the question actually got us into more trouble.

We learned that the word, "Why?" is like a hand grenade. There's no way to win when it's lobbed into a conversation. The word asks one thing, (literally focusing on the situation), but the tone asks another, (what makes YOU such a problem and so irritating). On the surface, objectively speaking, "Why?" is looking for information. But underneath that objective question, there is a question asked by the tone of the word - an attacking question about the person being asked.

So, which did we learn to answer? The literal question that looked for a reason? Or the inferred question associated with the tone? We learned to answer both!

Don't Ask "Why?"

We learned to defend our SELF while attempting to answer the "why" part of the question. But the content of our answer was skewed to help defend self.

As our heart rate jumped and sweat began to form, we got better at crafting an answer that would protect ourselves while giving rationalizing, justifying reasons for the violation. It became a conditioned response: Hear the question "Why?", automatically defend self.

Now, there *is* something you can do if you truly want to know what happened. If you are the "why-er" in an interaction, just don't use that word. Without the word, there is no conditioned response, so you get clearer answers.

Psychologically speaking, when a person hears the word, "why," it triggers the place in the brain that houses a parent-child, rationalizing, defensive mindset. Simply changing the wording of the question, even if your tone stays the same (which I wouldn't recommend), triggers ANOTHER place in the listener's brain - a place with no conditioned response. With the following wording of the question, the person's mind will go to a place of truth. They think about what truly DID happen, and will be more likely to give you an answer that is clear and legitimate.

Do this: replace the word "why" with words like, *"*what prevented..." or, "how it is that..." or "tell me more about...." These types of words are far more useful in getting an answer you can more specifically respond to.

A parent can ask, "Johnny, what prevented you from cleaning your room? You said you would." A teacher can ask, "How is it that your homework didn't get done?" And a boss can say, "Tell me the reason the report wasn't finished on time." All of those questions trigger a better place in the listener's mind. They don't evoke a conditioned response of mixed emotions so the listener will be more apt to give you an honest answer.

The nudge, then? Take "why" out of your vocabulary and you will start getting the real truth of the matter.

Notice the difference when you hear the question, "What prevented you from being here on time?" compared to "WHY WERE YOU LATE?"

Here's another example, referring to this Nudge: Do you get it? If not, WHY DON'T YOU!?!? (See how that feels?)

ACHIEVE MORE OF THE TRUTH BY NOT ASKING "WHY?"

Achievement Nudge #16

Frying Pans

Psychologists, counselors, and therapists all say the same thing; when you criticize someone, you are most likely referring to something that's also inside of you. This could be a real eye-opener if we are courageous enough to listen to ourselves.

I guess the old saying is true, "When you're pointing a finger at someone else, there are three fingers pointing right back at yourself!" And if the psychologists are right (and I've learned that they are…), all we have to do to understand what we don't like about ourselves is to listen to how we criticize others. This story illustrates one of the many times in my life where I experienced this truth.

Many years ago, Joann and I rented a houseboat on Lake Shasta to celebrate our honeymoon. We rented a rather modest, somewhat Spartan houseboat that had the company name on the side and a big painted number – 58. You could tell from across the lake that we were in a rental boat. But that's ok. Though we like the nicer things in life, this time we weren't renting luxury, we were renting togetherness.

One evening we beached the boat for the night and decided to use our blow-up boat to explore the nearby coves. I labored over a hand pump and finally got the plastic, yellow boat to hold enough air to keep us afloat. But then…I realized I had forgotten the oars.

Joann suggested I use frying pans. Very creative I thought, so I followed her suggestion. She got into the back of the little boat and I laid face-down on the pointy bow with a frying pan in each hand. Pulling on both sides of the boat at the same time, I paddled, or rather "pulled" us along. Though blowing up the boat was a bit of a chore, "frying-panning" it was hard work, too. But I swallowed my irritation and the wishing that we had a powerboat so we could enjoy our togetherness. After all, that was what this was about anyway, right? Besides, the frying pans worked quite nicely.

Proud of her resourcefulness and chuckling at my implementation of it, Joann sipped a beverage while we explored. As we rounded a corner we saw six houseboats all lined up in a row. I used the frying pans to hold us steady while we looked more closely at them.

The one on the far left was a beautiful, luxurious, houseboat. It was well appointed and had evidence of all the latest gear. Tied to the house boat was a hot, tricked-out, competition ski boat, and tied to that was a couple of high-powered jet skis. The only place THEY needed frying pans was in the kitchen.

That first boat was filled with luxurious, expensive toys. Everything on it reeked of money. And it was the same down the line. The second, third, fourth and fifth boats where just as opulent as the first one. But the sixth boat? That boat was different. It was tied into the group, but was certainly not like any of the others.

The sixth boat was a bit shabby. If the owner told me it was hand-made I would have believed it. It stood out in stark contrast to the other five boats. THIS houseboat didn't have the fancy paint job, nor did it have the two (or three) stories the other boats enjoyed. Instead of a competition ski boat tied to it, there was an open, metal fishing boat with a small outboard motor. In place of a jet ski there was a blue, plastic paddle boat.

With "Number 58" silhouetting me from behind, I propped myself up from the bow of our yellow, plastic, drug-store-bought, blow-up boat and pointed to that sixth houseboat with my frying pan, waving it in the air and saying with a sarcastic tone…, "Look at those wanna-be's!"

Then I dug those frying pans into the water and brought our blow-up boat safely back to Number 58. The only thing left to do was choose between frozen lasagna and Salisbury steak for dinner. It WAS our anniversary after all.

ACHIEVE AWARENESS OF WHAT YOU THINK OF YOU BY PAYING ATTENTION TO WHAT YOU THINK OF OTHERS

Achievement Nudge

Struggle In Your Mind

There is a power struggle between your conscious mind and your subconscious mind. Which one wins tells me whether you are living in your past, or are free to grow and achieve new things now and in your future.

Your conscious mind is powerful, but your subconscious mind **FEELS** more powerful. You know what I mean. I'm sure you have felt the struggle if you are trying to lose weight, break a habit or achieve something new.

Your subconscious mind controls 90% of what's going on in your body and that power is beyond your awareness. How your body is functioning, your attitude, even your thoughts we call "self-talk," are all being controlled by your subconscious mind.

But your subconscious only has the repertoire of choices that come from your past. That's its default, so that's your default.

I've demonstrated this in workshops where I'll tell someone I'm going to shake their hand. I ask them permission to shake their hand. After they give that permission, I walk toward them telling them I am going to shake their hand. Then I reach out with my LEFT hand to shake theirs. And since they are expecting me to use my right hand, they freeze.

Their mind literally goes into an altered state as their conscious and subconscious mind battles for a few seconds. The conscious mind sees my left hand raised. But the subconscious draws from the past and KNOWS it's supposed to raise the right hand when someone wants to shake hands. The subconscious habit of "hand shaking protocol" temporarily overpowers and paralyzes the conscious mind's view of what's going on, and the choice to raise their left hand.

And the subconscious mind will actually win for a few seconds. The person will literally sit stunned for about 4 seconds and may even raise their right hand then freeze in that position during those seconds. Eventually the conscious mind takes over and we shake left hands.

Every new and different achievement is like this. It will be hindered with the weight of your subconscious mind's power…that is, UNLESS you recognize its power and UNTIL you teach your subconscious mind something new.

Here's the secret power that can manage this process: Though there is a power struggle, the conscious mind, manifested in the ***power of choice,*** is indeed stronger.

The subconscious is so powerful in certain situations that it can overpower the conscious, especially in stronger responses we are trying to change. If this is happening to you, you may need a reminder that we DO have choice so your conscious mind has a chance to get engaged and choose.

The very existence of a reminder creates the ***awareness that you HAVE a power of choice,*** then can automatically lead you to a new, conscious choice. Here's how you can create a reminder.

Many years ago I needed to learn to relax. I went to a biofeedback therapist who showed me how to relax. But my subconscious mind would take over so quickly and put me right back into the stress-filled, fast-paced, adrenaline-flowing way of living. A simple little exercise managed my subconscious mind by creating a reminder so my conscious mind could engage.

I bought some stickers, little Avery blue dots. I held the sheet of dots in my hand and spent a few minutes visualizing my desired choice while focusing on the dots. This "anchored" the choice to relax to the blue dots.

I then placed blue dots in as many places as I could so I would run into them throughout the day – my car's rear view mirror, the phone, my computer, a portfolio I carried…and it worked.

Every time I saw a blue dot, it reminded me that I had a choice as to how I would respond to stress, and I rather automatically chose to relax. My shoulders would drop, I took a deep breath and I relaxed.

Eventually, my subconscious learned too, and I didn't have to make a conscious choice anymore. My conscious mind trained my stubborn subconscious "stuck in the past" mind by using reminders coupled with the power of choice.

The nudge: Think about what you want to achieve. Use your power of choice to make conscious choices. Then train your subconscious mind by using some sort of reminder. If you don't train your subconscious mind, you'll continuously experience the power struggle that, in and of itself, can defeat you.

Now here's a thought. Who is observing the conscious and subconscious mind and choosing which one wins? Hmmm…. maybe THAT part of you has even more power?!?!

ACHIEVE GREATER FREEDOM BY MANAGING YOUR SUBCONSCIOUS MIND, REMINDING IT OF YOUR CONSCIOUS MIND'S CHOICE

Achievement Nudge #18

A Map Isn't the Territory

The map is not the territory, the menu is not the meal, and worry is an invention of the mind.

"Worry" is something we learn, not something we are born with. Animals, babies, toddlers all have the innocence to more happily and healthfully live in the moment. If they feel something that is unpleasant or fearful, their response can change quickly – as quickly as the moment changes.

Worry and anxiety seems to be an invention of our mind that we learn from others...and learn it after we are 8 years old.

The National Association of School Psychologists says that before the age of 8, children are anxious about specific, identifiable events such as an animal they see, being in the dark; or localized situations like the ubiquitous monster under the bed. After that age they unfortunately begin to worry about future events like an upcoming school play. They'll worry about issues that can't be controlled such as what others think of them. Or they worry about self-esteem and identity issues; about not feeling worthy or whether or not they will be liked and loved.

How much better off we would be if we could regain our innocence.

Achievement Nudge

One way to do that is to realize what is embedded in these truths: The map is not the territory and the menu is not the meal.

After we are 8 years old, we begin creating mental maps of reality that are often not accurate. Our anxiety creates a map of what we THINK reality is or will be. Then we live and respond based on our **map**; not on the **reality of the territory**.

We live as if there is no bridge across the river because our mental map doesn't show the one that is really there. Or we still use a distorted map from our early childhood days. We haven't bought a new one that accurately depicts current reality…sort of like using an old map of Texas to navigate in Virginia. (*The silly things we do in our mind…*)

The menu analogy is slightly different. What we are looking at is not OUR mental map; it is a batch of words **someone else has given us** to describe the experience. But the words that describe the food may or may not be accurate when it comes to the actual experience of eating the food.

Most of us respond from the map and eat from the menu – we don't live in the territory or experience the meal. This is what can cause so much stress, ill health and a lot of our problems.

This nudge is to, first, get you to live in the territory, not the map. It's to get you to look around at what's real, what's now, what you can feel under your feet, what is true and real…RIGHT NOW, and NOT to live in the made up map.

This nudge is also to get you to use the menu as a guide not as the absolute truth. It's only ONE set of choices that someone has given you in a certain situation. Instead, YOU be the chef. You create any meal you want! Don't be limited by someone else's menu. Create your own.

When you look in the mirror, you are probably looking at someone who is living in a map and a menu. But when you look in the eyes of a child, you are looking at a reflection of a person who lives in the "now".

Regain YOUR innocence by enjoying the moment of being tickled – not worrying about whether or not you will ever be tickled again. Fear only the monster under the bed, IF there is, indeed, a monster under your bed – and certainly not the ones that may or may not materialize in the future. Enjoy cuddling in the arms of the ones who love you today – don't worry about being loved tomorrow.

ACHIEVE GREATER PEACE BY EXPERIENCING WHAT IS REAL

Achievement Nudge

Achievement Nudge #19

Kissing and Hugging

This nudge looks at the science of kissing called philematology, and is going to nudge you to do more kissing. I suppose you're liking this nudge already, aren't you!

Putting lips together in a "kiss" (from the Germanic "kuss", probably based on how a kiss sounds), supposedly started in a very unromantic way. Philematolgist scientists theorize that it started with primates pre-chewing food for their babies then putting their mouths together to transfer the food. I'm happy we don't do that anymore. But learning to lock lips as a result of that feeding habit has become a great byproduct.

There are ceremonial kisses, Hollywood air kisses; even the Judas Kiss of Death, and a peck that revived a princess in a fairytale. But the kiss we are looking at in this nudge is when two people's lips come together in affection or passion. This kind of connection is provocatively powerful, and it's probably because of the amount of nerve endings in our lips. Lips are 100 times more sensitive than the tips of our fingers. Not even our genitals have as much sensitivity as our lips. (Lighten up; this is science!)

Scientists say that kissing transmits a ton of internal and external information that can have relationship consequences. A "first kiss" can stop a relationship dead in its tracks. Further, the type and frequency of kissing can certainly be a tell-tale sign of how a relationship is going.

New research says that kissing unleashes many chemicals that govern stress, motivation, social bonding and sexual stimulation. Increases in oxytocin, (the feel good hormone), and a decrease in cortisol, (the stress reducing hormone), both are results of kissing.

And if you kiss while holding hands or hugging it's even better. Research showed that blood pressure and heart rate decreased while holding hands or hugging.

Now let's talk a minute about the "French Kiss", then I have a warning for you men. The French Kiss didn't originate in France. The term began to be popular in America in about 1923 when soldiers returning from posts in France began to speak of it – and demonstrate it.

French kissing involves all 35 muscles in the face. A pucker kiss involves only two. And when the tongue is involved, a small bit of testosterone is transferred from the man to the woman helping her to feel more aroused or passionate.

But here's the warning to men who can be a bit more aggressive when beginning to kiss. Men tend to want to initiate the "French Kiss" more quickly than woman. BUT…a woman can have her oxytocin DECREASE if there isn't a bit of romance or gentleness in the initial approach of a passionate kissing session. Slow down guys!

Kissing and Hugging

And here's an interesting fact: Approximately two thirds of people tip their head to the right when they kiss. Scientists say this probably started with breast feeding. Since most women are right handed, they are more comfortable holding their baby with their left arm leaving their right arm free to do other things. This causes the baby to tip its head to the right to nurse.

So go tip your head to the right and kiss! When you do you'll receive many, MANY benefits. You can help reduce stress, lower your blood pressure, decrease your heart rate – even lose weight. No really, you can!

I've learned that kissing burns about 6.4 calories a minute. For perspective, a Hershey's kiss contains 26 calories, which takes five minutes of walking – or about four minutes of kissing – to burn off. Which exercise do you choose? I prefer to kiss!!

XOXOXO

ACHIEVE GREATER HAPPINESS, LESS STRESS AND BETTER HEALTH…BY KISSING

Achievement Nudge

Achievement Nudge #20

Good News Re: Bad Habits

I have some good news about your bad habits. Having a bad habit shows you have personal power. I'll tell you what I mean.

We all have habits. The way you brush your teeth every day, stopping by that coffee shop every morning for a Mocha, eating too much dessert every night for dinner – all can be habits that formed over time.

But the good news is this: a habit is a habit, no matter what it looks like. Whether you think of it as a good habit or a bad habit, it's still a habit. From a scientific, objective point of view, both good and bad habits look the same. BOTH have the same sequential process that plays out in your mind and behavior.

Now, this is good news because it proves...

If you have developed a bad habit, you can develop a good one!

A habit is a habit.

Let's look at how habits are formed. In very, very simple terms, a habit forms when the following happens repeatedly. (1) Something triggers a thought. (2) The thought triggers an action. (3) That action gives you a reward. That's it. And the reward is the key. It makes the behavior stick.

And, yes, bad habits give reward too, even if that "reward" is deeply hidden. The habit of procrastination can give rewards like being in control, or attention, or avoiding pain, or… "something" that has a benefit for you. All habits give reward.

Now, this "reward thing" is why breaking a bad habit is so hard. Often, we focus on the consequences to give us incentive to break a bad habit. The wagging finger messages are these: Your habit of nightly dessert will cause you to gain weight. You're going to get criticized if you procrastinate. You will get lung cancer if you smoke.

But consequences aren't typically enough of an incentive to overpower the reward. The reward is the key. We need to find a different habit that gives a different reward. For example, focusing on the reward of living a longer, healthier life with your family has far more power to break the smoking habit than focusing on the consequence of lung cancer.

But why is developing a good habit hard too? It's usually because we are typically not working on the good habit in isolation. Instead, we are trying to develop a good habit to eliminate a bad one. And that's HARD working on both at the same time, especially since the bad habit with ITS reward has been around longer and is more deeply entrenched.

This nudge is to educate you a little about habits, but it's more to nudge you to give yourself some credit for developing your bad habits. They are usually quite strong so they took some personal power, tenacity and maybe even hard work to build. Kudos to you! "Well done!" This proves you have personal power.

And it proves if you want to break a bad habit by creating a good habit, I KNOW you can do it. You've already proved you can.

A habit is a habit! All you need to do is figure out the reward that the bad habit is giving, choose a better reward, then figure out what behavior will get you that new reward. Get a trigger to remind you to repetitively implement your chosen behavior, and you've done it. You've created a new habit, you strong person, you!

And by the way, if you've read this far, I'm REALLY glad you have developed the habit of reading the Achievement Nudge every week. Well done! A habit is a habit.

ACHIEVE GOOD HABITS BY LEARNING FROM YOUR BAD HABITS

Achievement Nudge

 Achievement Nudge #21

Loss Aversion

We are constantly and consistently focusing on the positive, at least that's what we're trying to do in these nudges and in our life. But to do that, we need to avoid a natural motivator tucked away in the recesses of our subconscious mind.

Deep within us there is a dynamic called "Loss Aversion." Avoiding loss seems to be a stronger motivator for our deep subconscious brain than achieving gains. Here's an example of this loss aversion.

I read a study about professional golfers. The research focused on 2.5 million putts, comparing the success of golfers putting for a birdie compared to putting for a par. *(Stat keepers in sports are wonderful resources for research scientists).*

When you golf, putting for a birdie is perceived as going ***ahead*** one stroke. Putting for a par is perceived as NOT getting a bogie and you go ***backwards*** one stroke. Get a birdie, get a gain. Get a par, avoid a loss. Now...in which situation do you think the golfers were more successful?

The study found that the golfers were 3.6% more accurate with par putts than birdie putts. They seemed to be better at getting a par to avoid the loss of a stroke, than they were at getting a birdie to go ahead one stroke. This is loss aversion at work.

The power of avoiding loss over the power of achieving gains is all around us. Buying insurance, preventing relationship difficulties, education to avoid being jobless, achieving a smaller goal to avoid the loss of not achieving a larger goal…all are examples of what can subconsciously motivate us.

This dynamic also means that something negative captures our attention more quickly and more strongly than something positive. An angry face stands out in a crowd of happy faces more than a happy face does in a crowd of angry faces…and a cherry in a bowl of cockroaches is less powerful and captures less attention than one cockroach in a bowl of cherries.

Loss Aversion is a powerful motivator. Biologists confirm that in a territorial battle, the animal who is defending its territory most always wins. That animal is fighting to avoid loss while the new animal is fighting to achieve gain.

Here is another example of the motivating effect of Loss Aversion: If a retail store lowers prices, it can actually lose current customers who perceive a loss because they just paid a higher price for the same item. Current customers have the motivation to ***not buy more*** because they don't want to lose if the store lowers prices again. In fact, THAT motivation in the current customers can be stronger than the gain achieved from new customers who buy because of the lower price.

What do you do about this? First, you can't fight it. No amount of covering, ignoring, or avoiding a natural law or truth will make it go away. Loss Aversion is embedded deep within your subconscious mind. It's not going away. It has to be managed.

But the good news is this: Managing Loss Aversion is rather simple in concept...even though it may be difficult in practice. Here's how you do it:

1. Understand and acknowledge it

2. Use your power of choice to determine what you will focus on and what you will do about it

Don't let a pre-programed biological drive control you. Instead, let your higher self use your power of choice to determine your attitude and behavior. As you look at how you are living life, challenge anything you are doing or feeling that is not comfortable. Ask yourself, "What makes me do or feel this?" Your power of choice is the key...to everything - even Loss Aversion.

In fact, your power of choice, especially the **POWER of CHOICE** that is motivated by love, is the most powerful force there is.

ACHIEVE A POSITIVE OUTCOME BY MANAGING YOUR TENDENCY TO AVOID LOSS

Achievement Nudge

Achievement Nudge #22

Sunk Cost Effect

Ever wonder why you hold on to something longer than you know you should - even when it's going south? It's probably because of a psychological condition called the "Sunk Cost Effect."

The "Sunk Cost Effect" is when you invest in something, but it's an investment you can't recover. It could be the time it takes to develop a new relationship, the purchase of a timeshare, the time and energy it takes to start a new direction or venture. But then the situation sours and you continue to hold on to it, even if you experience MORE loss. What's going on?

Some would call it commitment. But, it's probably not. More often, it's what psychologists, economists and scientists call the "Sunk Cost Effect."

Psychologists say we are more motivated by loss aversion than we are by attaining gain. Holding on, then, to that relationship, timeshare, direction or decision, even though it has soured, gives the illusion that we have not lost the initial investment...even if we would gain more, in the long run, by letting go.

Here's an example. You buy an expensive ticket for a concert. When the night of the concert comes, you don't feel like going at all. You'd be happier staying home, sitting by a cozy fire with a cup of hot tea, and reading a good book. But what do you do? You go to the concert. You've already sunk money into a ticket you can't recoup, so you persist in your decision to go.

Another example: A country continues in a war that is unlikely to be won, even though additional lives will be lost. Stepping away from the war would keep additional soldiers from perishing. But to leave the war would make the initial loss of lives unbearable. This is the power of the "Sunk Cost Effect." More lives are lost to make the initial investment of lost lives more tolerable. So sad.

And weird, huh? Yet, it occurs all the time, for all of us. Let's say you invest in the training of a new hire. That is a "sunk cost loss" that can't be recouped. If the new hire doesn't work out, a leader may still hold on to that employee much longer than appropriate. To fire this employee and start over makes the initial investment seem like a bigger loss.

It's no different when purchasing a new phone system, Internet provider, or even choosing one of two paths in the woods - all can become the stage for "the Sunk Cost Effect," where we continue longer than we want and "throw good money after bad."

What to do? Take an inventory of your life. Look honestly at everything. Use the phrase, "This is in my life because... (Blank)." Then fill in the

Sunk Cost Effect

blank. If you don't like your answer, question whether you are holding on because of the "Sunk Cost Effect."

If you are holding on because of that effect, the only way you'll be able to let go is to separate your new decision from the initial investment...MUCH easier said than done. Your decision must be made while looking forward. Continuing to look backward at your initial investment of time, money, energy, or even lives...will tend to perpetuate the sense of loss of that initial investment.

The "Sunk Cost Effect" is neither logical nor objective, and it actually causes you to lose more. It's as strange as this: I ask for $10.00. Later, I tell you I can't pay you back, but if you'll loan me $20.00, I might be able to use that money to buy and sell some product to pay back the entire $30.00. You give me the $20.00. Now you are even more invested. Later still, I tell you I can't pay back the $30.00, but if you give me another $15.00, I can TRY to get and sell some more products to pay you all the money back....The "Sunk Cost Effect" determines how far you'll go down this trail.

Now, if you're having a hard time with this nudge, let's play it out together so you can see how it works. Send me $10.00, OK? I'll give you the next step when I get your check.

Achievement Nudge

ACHIEVE GREATER RETURN BY LETTING GO OF WHAT YOU'VE ALREADY LOST

Achievement Nudge #23

Spooky Action at a Distance

Got a problem? Maybe some Voodoo can help.

Einstein called it "spooky action at a distance." In fact he never came to accept the concept I'm going to talk about. His sticking point was "Quantum Entanglement," a mind blowing, yet proven concept in quantum physics where two particles separated by a universe of distance, are connected in such a way that if one is affected, the other is instantaneously affected too.

In our everyday experience, if Jake lives in New York and Janice lives in California, they are separated by distance. Something has to traverse that distance for them to connect or be affected by each other. A telephone, letter, car, plane…something has to be used by Jake to connect and affect Janice. This is not so in quantum physics.

Over the past 20 years, multiple quantum physics experiments have proven without a doubt that, (1) everything is symmetrical and exists in relationship – nothing exists alone, (if there's a Jake there has to be a Janice), and (2) If you affect one part in the relationship, then the other part in that relationship is **INSTANTANEOUSLY** affected too, even if separated by light-years of distance.

Achievement Nudge

This is just like the scenario in the old black and white scary movies. An African Voodoo Witchdoctor, sitting in his hut in the middle of the jungle, can stick a pin into a doll and cause the handsome, smiling explorer enjoying his "welcome home cocktail party" to writhe in pain. "Spooky action at a distance." (Hmmm…. Maybe Voodoo Witchdoctors were the first quantum physicists???)

Einstein had a problem with this because the information between the two would be experienced at speeds faster than the speed of light, which, according to his relativity theory, was impossible.

Yet Juan Yin and a team of scientists from the University of Science and Technology of China in Shanghai conducted an ingenious experiment that clocked this information exchange at speeds of "at least four orders of magnitude faster than the speed of light." That's approximately 744,000 miles per second as compared to the speed of light which is 186,000 miles per second. (They say "at least" because of the limitations of their equipment. And they admit, the affect could still be "instantaneous.")

If we look at Jake and Janice in "quantum physics entanglement" terms, Jake could feel an itch in New York, Janice immediately senses the itch in California. Janice scratches the itch. Jake feels instant relief. Is this a bit weird? Maybe so. But that's how it works at the quantum level. But, how does all of this give us a practical nudge? Hold on. I'm hoping to affect you instantaneously now…

Since everything exists in a logical and symmetrical relationship, if there is a problem there must be a solution. It's symmetrical. The very instant there is a problem, at that instant there must be a solution. You can't have one without the other.

It follows then; if you affect one, you will automatically and instantaneously affect the other. Interact with the problem in some way, it changes the solution. Interact with the solution, it changes the problem. And THERE is the focus of this nudge. WHERE...DO... YOU...FOCUS? With what side of the symmetry do you engage?

The scientists stood between Jake and Janice, the two separated particles, and conducted the experiment. When they focused on one and affected it in some way, the other was automatically and instantaneously affected too.

In my metaphor, YOU are the scientist. If Jake is the problem in New York and you keep focusing on Jake, interacting with Jake, amplifying the effects of Jake, well then...Janice will be affected by experiencing more of the problem. However...*(you're getting this, right?)*, if Janice in California is the solution and you focus on her, Jake gets immediate relief.

And it doesn't matter how far the solution seems from the problem. In quantum physics terms, distance is irrelevant. Ignore the distance between the problem and the solution. Focus only on the solution. When you do, the problem has to be instantaneously and positively affected. It can't be otherwise. It's science. It's common sense *(albeit, "uncommon" common sense!)*

Now, I am left with two conclusions. First, I suppose I believe in Voodoo. (wink)

Second, if Jake in New York is the problem, and Janice in California is the solution, and I'm going to focus on the solution, AND distance doesn't matter,...I think I'll move Janice and the solution further west... say, to Hawaii. Every solution is better there.

Aloha, Jake!

ACHIEVE THE FINDING OF A SOLUTION THROUGH QUANTUM ENTANGLEMENT

 Achievement Nudge #24

Rules Give Fun and Freedom

Freedom doesn't mean "no rules." In fact, without rules you can't have freedom, or happiness and or fun.

There is some interesting research surrounding the psychology of "play" and how it parallels the dynamics of living life. Two things struck me as I looked at it.

First, the prevalence of playing games, in both humans and animals. Every culture throughout the history of our world shows clear evidence of playing games. Animals played games too. There was one example of a game where monkeys rolled coconuts downhill to see who could roll one the farthest.

Observations from this research showed that all humans play with each other. They NEED to play. YOU need to play.

A second learning from the studies had to do with rules. It may seem like common sense, but it was clear; you have to have rules in order to play. But more than that, rules are absolutely necessary to make you *happy* to play the game, AND to make the game *fun*. A simple thought experiment proves this point.

Achievement Nudge

If you are playing baseball, basketball, ping pong ball, soccer, poker, Candyland, even "I spy" with your kids in the car – the game needs rules or nobody wants to play. And, when someone doesn't want to play by the rules, or even plays by different rules, we aren't very happy. The game isn't fun anymore, and we don't want to play with that person. Rules make us happy and give us fun while we play the game.

You can't get together and play ANY game with no rules. You can't play the game of "life" with no rules either.

Fletcher Christian found this to be true. He put Captain Bligh on a long boat in the middle of the ocean after the mutiny on the ship "Bounty." He and his band of men and women then found the lonely Pitcairn Island and started a new life. They burned the ship and said, "We will now live in complete happiness. No rules. Every man can live his own life in whatever way he chooses." But the "no rule" thing? It didn't work.

It wasn't long before there were arguments over supplies and fights over places to live. Theft, deceit, rape and fear became common. When murders became common too, Fletcher Christian realized he needed to do something. He gathered everyone together and formed an alliance with rules they agreed to live by. Thereafter, they had peace and happiness. The rules made the game of life fun again.

Even nature has rules. When those rules are broken, typically by some life-form, like humanoids messing with those rules, it has global consequences.

Rules Give Fun and Freedom

This particular observation leads to a more alarming one – it seems that humans are the only ones in the universe who break rules and create these global consequences – but that's another story.

Rules not only give the game of life happiness and fun, they also provide freedom. That's right, rules give freedom.

It's a bit of an irony, but I can illustrate it by asking you to think about driving your car. You have a ton of freedom there, don't you? You can drive it anytime you want, anywhere you want, any way you want – well…except on the wrong side of the road, or way over the speed limit, or the wrong way on a one way street, or on someone else's lawn, or…. You see what I mean?

True freedom is living within rules, not without rules. An echo from the truth in an old saying comes to mind, "Your freedom ends where my nose begins."

Then why are we drawn to the rebel, the stories about the person who bends the rules, stretches the rules, even breaks the rules?

It's because we want freedom, and fall into the trap that, "Freedom means NO RULES." But, like Fletcher Christian learned, that's a misconception. It's important to have freedom. It's a mistake to tie that concept to a life with no rules.

In real life, when we are in relationship with another person (or many persons for that matter), there have to be rules or we won't be happy. We won't have fun. And in truth, we won't even be able to play the game.

Now, here is a weird twist on the psychology of "play."

Who is the winner when everyone plays by the rules? Everyone! Even in a game like football, the so-called spectators, the "winner" of the game, and the "loser," actually ALL win when everyone plays by the rules.

Though one team isn't happy about their score, they still are happy to have played the game, and even had fun doing so. If they didn't, they wouldn't come back better, stronger, happier and ready to have MORE fun in the next game!

True freedom is living within rules, not without rules. When you are in relationship – with a friend, a spouse, a teacher, a club, an employer, or whomever – it is important that you know what the rules are. Then play by those rules.

That's especially important when you are in relationship with a larger body of people, like your community. If you break significant rules there, you could end up in one of those fun houses. You know…the place with LOTS of rules so there must be tons of fun. It's called a prison.

ACHIEVE MORE HAPPINESS AND FUN WHEN YOU PLAY BY THE RULES

Achievement Nudge

Achievement Nudge #25

Calves and Beauty Queens

Let me tell you what I learned about "valuing" SELF. It started by comparing calves on the farm with a Hollywood beauty pageant.

When I was very young, my cousins, brothers and I would take calves from our farm in Ferndale, California to the county fair to show them. We'd "pretty 'em up," as my uncle would say, and get them ready to walk around a ring for judges to decide who would get the blue ribbon.

I'll never forget coming into the house one day after taking care of the calves in the barn. Mom was watching a Miss America Pageant. I saw a bunch of women who had been "prettied up" walking around for judges to decide who would get the winning ribbon.

Even at my young age I wondered about this. Was this right? Was it even fair? – for calves OR for women? Who are these judges that can hand out a valuation like this anyway? What criteria do they use? What criteria can they use?

Later in life, during my Master's Program, the subject of how we value ourselves came up. I remembered the calves and the pageant and started asking the same questions I did as a young boy. During the next number of years, I began to formulate some thoughts and conclusions as I found some answers. I'll tell you what I discovered.

There are two types of criteria we use to value (or evaluate) most everything; "performance-based" criteria and "existence-based" criteria. I also learned that it's a real problem when we mix them up and use the wrong criteria.

What is the difference between the two? Let's look at performance-based criteria first. We are intimately acquainted with that one.

How do you know whether an apple tree is a good apple tree or not? You can tell by the fruit. If it produces good apples, it's a good tree. It doesn't matter how the tree looks, how big it is or even its location. Good apples? It's a good tree.

Likewise, you cannot tell how good a bakery is by looking at its equipment. You have to taste the bread. You cannot tell how much a weight lifter can lift by looking at his muscles. He has to lift the weight. This is a valuation from "performance-based" criteria. Lift more weight, you are a better weight lifter.

"Existence-based" criteria is different. Let's imagine you're in the middle of the ocean. A lifeboat would be nice, right? If one comes along, are you going to determine its "value" based on its color, its length or how it performs? No! Its value rests in the fact that it exists.

Think about the air you breathe – sure, you could focus on whether or not it is good quality air, but the REAL "value" is in whether it exists or not. Is their air to breathe? That's the bottom line question!

What about life itself. You can have a different quality of life, a different length of life, a different type of life – but life itself? Its value is in whether it exists or not. What you do with it comes after.

That's the difference between the two. A performance-based criterion is about how something ***does***. An existence-based criterion is valued on whether or not something ***IS***.

Most of us have learned to use performance-based criteria to value our SELF, but this is just wrong. Doing this is like valuing the life boat based on how it looks or what it can do. Its existence is the criteria, not its performance. A log is just as good as a yacht if it is their to save your life.

You can use performance-based criteria to evaluate how well you ***DO*** something, but it is not to be used to value you as a human ***BEING***. You are valuable because you ***are***, not because of what you ***do***.

How do you use existence-based criteria to value yourself? Simply… and I mean SIMPLY…do this: Look in the mirror, pinch yourself… have someone else pinch you. If you can see yourself or feel the pinch, then you are valuable. Why? Because you ARE THERE. You are valuable because you exist. THAT is existence-based criteria.

Now…if you are one who INSISTS on using performance-based criteria to judge the value of YOU, give me a call. I'll try to remember everything we did to the calves.

I think it started with a bath then moved to grooming the hair on the hide. We taught it how to hold it's head, and…oh yes…we cut the tail hair too. That was very important!

Surely these kinds of preparations will "pretty you up" and get you ready for those judges! But remember, your blue ribbon only lasts for this year. You're going to have to keep working, and working, and working to prepare for the never ending judges that will keep watching you walk around the ring. Whew….existence-based criteria is so much easier.

ACHIEVE BETTER PERSPECTIVE ON YOUR VALUE BY USING THE RIGHT CRITERIA

Achievement Nudge #26

Can You Lick Your Elbow?

It's a known fact; changing how you think is more powerful than changing what you do. In fact, changing how you think WILL change what you do.

When people hear they can't lick their elbow – most people try it. Some have even proven the "fact" wrong. There are YouTube videos of people with freakishly long (or some might say "wonderfully long") tongues who have proved that licking their elbow *is* possible!

However, when people hear, "you can't survive a jump from a 10-story building" – no one goes out and tries THAT! What's the difference? The difference is in two types of thought processes. I call these different types of thinking "Possibility Thinking" and "Probability Thinking."

When someone hears they can't lick their elbow, they may think, "Oh, yes I can" and try it; or "Is it really not possible?" and try it. They believe it may be possible. But...when someone hears about not surviving a 10-story jump, they believe that it is, indeed, not probable to survive, so won't try that. The first scenario engages Possibility Thinking, the second Probability Thinking.

Possibility Thinking believes that it is possible, that it might be possible, or that I can try it to see if it is possible. Probability Thinking goes with the stats, the research, the conclusion of a formula: 10 stories tall + my weight + the force of gravity = "ain't gonna make it!". It's not probable.

And it's important to know...

Probability Thinking takes away Possibility Thinking

When Thomas Edison was busy with over 10,000 tries to find what element might work in the light bulb, I'm absolutely sure he didn't fall into Probability Thinking. He didn't say, "This next try ***probably*** isn't going to work, but let's give it a go anyway." Falling into this kind of Probability Thinking would have limited his success. Instead he used Possibility Thinking – "Tungsten MIGHT work, it IS POSSIBLE! let's try that."...and, turns out, it was possible. It worked!

Now, there are times you *want* Probability Thinking. You don't want a doctor prescribing a medication with the words, "Hey, try this. It might work. It's possible….!" But using Probability Thinking when Possibility Thinking is available will limit you.

This nudge is for you to think about how you are going to think before you think. Anytime something is critical in your personal life, relationships or business – use Probability Thinking. Don't put you or anyone else at risk by "trying" something when your outcome is time sensitive or if your health, life or relationship will be jeopardized if it doesn't work.

However, don't limit yourself by Probability Thinking when it isn't warranted. Thoughts like "I'll probably fail" or "this probably won't work" will only hinder your achievement.

There is a saying around where we live associated with our beloved, 14,000 foot Mt. Shasta.

> *"Those who don't make it to the top will come down because of attitude, not altitude."*

They thought they probably wouldn't make it even though it was possible TO make it.

Don't mix up the two types of thinking. It will only limit your achievements. Use Probability Thinking when necessary. But use Possibility Thinking as much as possible. After all, if it's possible for someone…it's possible for you!

ACHIEVE MORE BY IMPLEMENTING "Possibility Thinking" over "Probability Thinking"

Achievement Nudge

Achievement Nudge #27

The Drip Or the Stream?

Seeing something differently may be all it takes to make things different.

I have been helping people become happier, healthier, and find more fulfillment for close to 40 years. And I've been the most successful at doing this by touching a person's eyes, not their hands – their perspective, not their effort.

The biggest, quickest, most long lasting change has NOT come from helping people know how to DO something differently; it has come from helping them SEE things differently. I call it a mind shift.

It's like this. If your only source of water is a slow drip, then that's where you go to quench your thirst. You can learn to be more positive as you do this, how to accept your lot in life, how to be happy that you even have water – but these are just coping mechanisms. You're still going to go to the drip because that's all you know.

You'll probably be frustrated from time to time, get discouraged, possibly even go thirsty now and then because of the hassle of getting water; but your attitude, behavior and direction all come from the "fact" that the drip is where you go to get water - and the belief that

THAT is your only choice.

However…what if I show you that there's a gushing stream in a place you didn't know about before? How long does it take you to change your attitude and behavior? How long does it take to start going to this new source of water? How much effort or training does it take to practice this new behavior and direction?

It takes no effort at all! The learning is quick, the change is instant, and the new way of doing things sticks for good. And it all comes about simply because you believe a new truth – you see things differently.

I find that most people get stuck "going to the drip" because we are slaves to our own mind. We draw from the only place we know of to get the "truths" to live our life.

Yet, putting your "mental musings" onto a situation is just that – YOUR mental musings. And YOUR perspective will dictate how you feel and what you think about the situation.

But how much of it is based on truth? On reality? How skewed is your perspective? The problem is, you may not know. The "drip" is all you know – and what you know is where you go!

So this nudge is to get more input about the things that bother you. If there is something that troubles you, that causes you fear, or makes you insecure in anyway, ask someone else (or a number of "someone elses") for their perspective. An experienced person, a book on the subject, even an objective critic can give you more information about the situation than what comes from the limitations in your mind. The "drip" may be all YOU know, but the person you're asking may know about a "gushing stream."

In my decades of helping people, this has been the case. People get stuck in their misery, because that's all they know. And I've seen too many people settle for that "drip" and live in that place way too long, when just around the corner is a "gushing stream." But I've also seen how a new perspective is all it takes to make HUGE changes.

So when it comes to YOUR happiness…in the purpose of your life, in the achievements of your work, in the fulfillment of your relationships…DON'T SETTLE for a drip. Find the gushing stream of a clearer perspective. It's deeply refreshing!

ACHIEVE REFRESHING CHANGE WITH A DIFFERENT PERSPECTIVE

Achievement Nudge

 Achievement Nudge #28

Driving a BMIR

Want to drive a BMIR?

Actually...you already are. But I'm not talking about a BMW. I'm talking about something in your brain.

First let's get something straight. You cannot...not think. That's right. It is impossible to turn off your mind. It is a persistent, insistent organ that influences every aspect of your existence. It is tireless, and always... ALWAYS...dictates how you feel and act at a given moment. You cannot turn it off.

Even meditative exercises, that are designed to quiet the mind, do so by asking you to focus on something like your breathing, or repeating a word (Ooommmmmmm). You quiet your mind from thinking about everything by choosing to think about one thing. And, you can't stop thinking about something by trying not to think about it.

If you are sick of thinking about a red monkey, you can't say, "I will NOT think of a red monkey!" The very moment you say that...well.... you think of the red monkey. You can actually **perpetuate** what you don't want to think about by trying not to think about it.

The only way to not think of a Red Monkey is to think about something else. Choosing to think about a green banana stops you thinking about a red monkey.

A related truth I've taught for years: You can't remember to forget. You have to forget to remember.

So, fact number one: You cannot, not think.

Fact number two: Every thought produces a response, an attitude and behavior associated with the thought. It's called a "BMIR" - a Behavioral Manifestation of an Internal Response. Whenever you think about something, it WILL create an internal response of some kind, and that response causes you to start driving the external manifestation of that response - the BMIR. Since you cannot not think, you cannot not have a response to that thought. You cannot not get into your BMIR and start driving it along the path your thought laid out for you. And often, it's a bumpy road!

So, what do you do if you don't like the condition of your BMIR, the road you're driving on? Dealing with the BMIR is not the answer. No amount of fussing with it is going to help much. Trying to make it look different by painting it a different color won't help. (I love the abundant lessons in this analogy...) Getting others to hop in and ride WITH you won't help. Your BMIR and the road you're driving on is going to be the same, no matter what, because of the "garage of thought" it came out of. What you do is the following... (and here comes some magic).

Driving a BMIR

To make a difference, you don't drive the BMIR back into the garage and choose another one. All you do is begin THINKING about another garage of thought and, POOF, everything changes. The BMIR you're driving instantly has a different feel. The sound system is playing a different song. The seat is more comfortable. And the scenery out of every window has changed.

Your BMIR - Behavioral Manifestation of an Internal Response - has changed because you changed the thought, not the vehicle of attitude and behavior launched by the thought.

This analogy is rich with lessons that I can't resist sharing. See if any of these apply to you.

1. Don't restore antique BMIRs.

2. Don't go to BMIR shows like "Hot August Nights" where there are a whole bunch of people showing off their BMIRs. It only perpetuates you wanting to keep yours.

3. Don't pick up hitchhikers to have someone to complain to about your road and your BMIR.

4. And seriously, IF you MUST drive a BMIR, for goodness sake, at least stop putting fuel in it.

ACHIEVE A BETTER JOURNEY BY DRIVING A DIFFERENT THOUGHT

Learn from the Dutch

Are you facing something insurmountable? Dutch people can teach you how to deal with it.

I wonder if there is anyone who knows how to face an insurmountable difficulty better than the Dutch people. I say that because (queue background story-telling music)…

Once upon a time, long, long ago, there was a land of people who grew to have too many people to fit into the amount homes they had. More and more children were being born. More young adults wanted to marry and strike out on their own…but all the houses were filled up.

New families and their children had nowhere to live in this growing country. And what's worse, there wasn't any more land on which to build houses. They were surrounded by the North Sea. It was a big problem.

One day, a young man named Kees was taking a bouquet of tulips to the girl he planned to marry. He wanted to give her a home, but knew there was no land left. His downcast eyes took sight of his wooden shoes. They reminded him of boats. And that reminded him of the ocean. And THAT sparked an idea. Spurred by the "no-problem-too-big" optimism that burns in the young, Kees turned and ran to the elders shouting, "I have the solution to not having enough land!"

"What is it?" said the discouraged and aged leaders. With unbridled enthusiasm Kees said, "LET'S JUST MOVE THE OCEAN!!!"

After a stunned silence, they looked at each other, a hint of a smile began to grow on the oldest elder, the spark spread to the others, then... strange as it seems, they took his suggestion and did it. They actually, literally, unbelievably, MOVED THE OCEAN! (Fade music).

So goes my made up legend about how Kees saved the Netherland. But the story IS based on fact. The Dutch people have been holding back the North Sea for over 2000 years. Using dikes and, originally, a windmill pumping system, they still hold back trillions of tons of water.

At present, over a quarter of their country's dry land is below sea level, and nearly 50% of the rest of their land is less than three feet above sea level. ***But they won!*** They moved the ocean.

Additionally, in case their solution stopped working, to prevent disaster, Amsterdam's buildings are all built on wooden poles. In fact, the Royal Palace, at Dam Square, is built on no less than 13,659 wooden poles. They solved the problem of no land, AND solved a future potential problem of dikes breaking.

Are you facing a seemingly impossible, challenge? If so, let's learn from the Dutch. First, be solution-oriented. Don't let anyone, no one, nobody, not one soul…take away your potential to find a solution. Read. Research. Talk to someone. Talk to everyone. Talk to the young. The situation is NOT impossible until you declare it so.

FIND A SOLUTION, then stick to the plan and you'll win just like the Dutch people did. And don't give up. The history of Holland's dike system is filled with failures. But it is just as much filled with people picking up their shovels…again. They found a solution, and never gave up on implementing it!

That's your nudge. YOU are in control of naming your situation. Is it an "impossible problem" or an "incredible challenge"? What you name it becomes what it is. And here's some good news. If you can turn the problem into a challenge, find a solution, and stick to the plan…YOU will be better for it. EVERY difficulty grows us. Come to think of it, it may have literally done so for the Netherlanders.

Dutch people are the tallest people in the world with an average height of nearly six feet. Maybe dealing with their "underwater" problem in such a positive and consistent way has literally grown them. Now, if the dike breaks, they can, most certainly, still keep their head above water.

ACHIEVE GROWTH FROM YOUR DIFFICULTIES

Achievement Nudge

Achievement Nudge #30

100-Year-Old Man

I sat with a 100-year-old man for the past two days. I've known him for about 45 years. He has a number of health problems, but his mind is as sharp as yours or mine. I don't know how much time he has left. We talked and cried together, as he is clearly realistic about his condition. I love this man. I am like a son to him and he needed me. I was honored to spend time with him.

Why am I telling you this? To set up a gentle nudge. But first let me tell you what I observed, and have observed, in this man, some of the characteristics of this "century-man."

> **He is positive.** He never has a negative word to say. In fact he even puts a positive spin on negative occurrences.

> **He is completely other-centered.** He is consistently more concerned about me and his caretakers than himself.

> **He is patient.** He never complains. Though he may speak clearly and firmly about a need, he never complains about what he can't have or do.

> **He takes things as they come.** He doesn't worry about tomorrow,

but lives in and for today. He is objective about his condition yet has his realism married to optimism. He says, "I'm not giving up but we need to be realistic. Let's just live each day as it comes."

He exhibits all of these characteristics and more. He is loving, cooperative, thankful and kind. And he is all of these things, all of the time. It's how he lives life.

When do you suppose he started living life like this? Did he start at 99, 97, 80, 79...When? One thing is for sure; he started living this way a long time ago. It started..well...at YOUR age.

What do I mean? Simply this: How you decide to live today is how you will live tomorrow. We don't typically backslide. Choose to buy a TV today, and your path to buy and watch that TV will be perpetuated unless you make a new choice. Choose to live life in a better way today - more kind, loving, positive - and tomorrow will be better; as will the days that follow.

Other than changes due to mental or physiological decline, people don't decide to be worse. So when YOU are 100, you'll be living out the choices you make at your age today.

Let's check it out. How ARE you living today? Would someone want to sit with you today if you had a bunch of health problems and were 100 years old? Would YOU want to sit with YOU?

If the answer is "no", mostly no, decidedly no, or repetitive no, no, no, -

you might want to consider making a different decision about how you live life today. And…if you don't want to make a different decision… well…you better get a dog.

ACHIEVE A BETTER TOMORROW BY PAYING ATTENTION TO YOUR CHOICES TODAY

Achievement Nudge

 Achievement Nudge #31

Ants, the Next Super Power

No matter where you are on this planet, there is a superpower all around you that few ever think about or acknowledge.

The superpower I am talking about is something that may surprise you. It is the common ant. These tiny creatures live all around us in vast numbers. We typically don't acknowledge them as a superpower or even understand their strength. Though individually, they are a millionth the size of a human, they outnumber us a million to one. There are so many ants in the earth, if you added up their total weight it would match the total weight of all humans on our entire planet. They are truly an impressive force of power.

"Are ants *truly* a superpower?" you ask. Scientists believe so. Their teamwork is incredibly resourceful. They can hold onto each other's bodies to create a bridge for other ants. They can use their bodies to melt snow and dry out their homes. Their organization and delegation is so impressive, military experts study them. When they are on the march, little can stand in their way.

There are so many fascinating, astounding facts about ants and their achievements; it just blows your mind. They hunt. They farm. They keep herds of other insects. Certain types of ants can run the equivalent

Achievement Nudge

of a 26 mile marathon, and can do it at a 4-minute-per-mile pace the entire time. They can endure higher heat than any other land animal. Their strength is way beyond what you'd expect from their size.

Yet, unless this superpower strolls across our kitchen floor, we give it no attention. It is completely out of our awareness…and that got me thinking. I wondered what else we are unaware of.

Immediately it came to me. I realized there is a superpower within each of us that we seem to be just as unaware of as the ant-superpower. It is the "power of choice manifested in decision." Few people claim this power. Fewer still use it. Here's how it works…

When facing a storm of negative attitude, or thoughts, or behavior, you can bring this power to life by saying, "This ends today!" When you say this, it is so powerful you can feel it. Starting a new path of positive pursuits with "This STARTS today!" can be just as powerful; just as fulfilling.

When your words are powered by choice and manifested in decision and behavior, there's not much that can stop you. Make one decisive decision today. You'll feel the amazing power.

And here's one more macro inspiration from a micro insect. Possibly one of the most astounding things about ants is this: When they decide to go somewhere, nothing can stop them. Ants have been known to eat an entire tethered horse that was in their way. There is no "stop" in their "go"; there is no doubt in their day; there is no hesitancy in their insistency; and there is no weakness in their power. Why? Because they use power of choice manifested in decision. And THAT, my friend, is truly a superpower.

ACHIEVE GREATER POWER BY TAPPING INTO A SUPER POWER THAT'S ALREADY IN YOU

Achievement Nudge

Achievement Nudge #32

Temptations

Temptations abound! What can you do about them?

More and more, scientists are getting to know us better and better. And the more we know, the more interesting, complex and strange we become.

We used to think that a temptation only fueled desire. We now know that our bodies also try to trick us into yielding to the temptation by manufacturing a state of anxiety at the thought of NOT fulfilling the temptation.

A 2005 study looked at the physiological responses of women who called themselves "chocolate cravers." When exposed to pictures of chocolate, those pictures not only ignited a strong desire for chocolate and the thought of pleasure at having it, the temptation also gave them a feeling of agitation, even loss of control and fear at the thought of not getting the chocolate. These women said, "Temptation is stressful!"

What can you do when you feel tempted, when you feel the assault on your desire AND your fear?

You can do three things. First, don't fight the temptation. Telling yourself over and over that you will NOT yield to the temptation works against you. Try repeating to yourself, "I will not think of an apple!" It doesn't work. Every time you say the phrase, you think of the apple. Every time you say, "I will not yield to this temptation," gives the temptation life.

So the first step is to own the temptation. Embrace it. Name it. Tell it like it is. "I am tempted to have some chocolate." Yielding to the fact that you have a temptation is not the same as yielding to the temptation itself. "Temptation" is not sin. In fact, calling out the temptation for what it is gives you power.

Second, make a definitive choice. State, out loud, your decision! "I am tempted to have chocolate, and I choose NOT to have chocolate." A decision is your second source of power.

Now notice something here; repeating, "I will not yield to the TEMPTATION," is subtly different than deciding, "I will not have CHOCOLATE." The first focuses on the temptation itself and, as mentioned earlier, actually gives it life. The second focuses on the content of the temptation. I do acknowledge, however, that saying, "I will have a piece of fruit rather than chocolate," is even better.

The key is this: If you make a decision about chocolate, that decision can vaporize the temptation about chocolate.

But know this, owning the temptation and making a decision doesn't necessarily stop the music. You may still hear the song; the melody of that well-played temptation you've heard too you many times. That's why you need step three.

After ownership and decisiveness, the third thing to do is focus on something else. Look at something else. Choose to think about something else. Do something else. Do anything to focus your mind and body away from the temptation. You can't fight the temptation head-on. You have to be as crafty as the temptation. And you don't need to refocus for very much time.

Most temptations don't have a long shelf life. For example, when a person stops smoking, the temptation to have a cigarette, though HUGE in its persuasive power, only lasts about three minutes.

So there you have it. When tempted, (1) own it, (2) make a decision about it, and (3) focus on something else.

Now...what do you do if YOU are the TEMPTER, tempting someone else?! Well...do the same thing. (1) own it, (2), make a decision about it, and (3) focus on something else. And one more thing?…shame on you!

ACHIEVE CONTROL OVER TEMPTATIONS BY OWNING THEM

Achievement Nudge

 Achievement Nudge #33

Do You Work? Or Do a Job?

Do you have a job? (If you do, congratulations, by the way…). What achievements do you focus on at work? What achievements SHOULD you focus on?

During the nearly 40 years we've been working with people who are employed, it's been consistent – few focus on the achievements that can really make a difference. Oh, sure…everyone "does their work" but they do it to get their "to do list" done, not to really make a sustainable, positive difference - and make themselves more valuable as a team member or leader.

Getting your work done is not as valuable as getting your job done

Want to make sure YOU are focusing on achievements that matter as you do your work within your job? Here's an exercise we designed that can do that. It's a simple exercise that causes you to focus on your highest priorities–but from different perspectives.

The instructions for this exercise are simple. Find a brief moment where you can close your eyes and have paper and pen in front of you. Then ask yourself the following three questions. Ask them in the sequence I give them to you, and treat them completely separately – do

NOT answer all three at once. Answer the questions in the context of the next week.

You can repeat the exercise using a "month" as the time frame and that may give you different results.

OK, here are the questions…

1. ***If I was the leader or manager of my team or department,*** what are the three most important priorities I would want the person in my role to achieve this next week?

2. ***If I was the leader of the company or organization,*** what are the three most important priorities I would want the person in my role to achieve this next week?

3. ***If I was an owner in this company and the only way I could take home money is when the company made money,*** what are the three most important priorities I would want the person in my role to achieve this next week?

The premise of these questions comes from the observation that many people are so busy doing their work that they don't do their job.

I'm defining "work" to include the many tasks that can fill up a day, and "job" as the set of achievements or outcomes that come from the responsibilities of your role.

Do You Work? Or Do a Job?

Whether a person is a leader, manager or team member, the focus is often quite micro. "I need to get these things done!" Instead of a more strategic thinking about priorities that are broader in perspective, and more beneficial in the outcomes.

The three questions are designed to get you to think about priorities within your "job," not within a "to do list" of work related tasks. The first question emphasizes the importance of working together with others as a team under a leader. The second question emphasizes the perspective of the "whole" team's achievement goals rather than your individual work. And the third question emphasizes the importance of doing things that are contributive to the continued profitability and sustainability of the company.

This exercise is always valuable in helping you think differently and avoid "busy work." Sometimes it is surprisingly beneficial in helping you see something that is right under your nose...something you've been missing that is a high priority and greatly leveraged toward success, even something that is more personally fulfilling.

Doing this exercise allows you to potentially see things that were hidden before because you were constantly putting out fires. But constantly doing the work of putting out fires may be indicative that something is wrong.

In real life, if the fire department notices that they are responding to fire, after fire, after fire, after fire...they don't default to getting more fire fighters to do more *"work"* of fire fighting. Instead, they focus on doing a more leveraged *"job"* of fire prevention. They stop and look for the arsonist.

ACHIEVE BEING MORE VALUABLE BY FOCUSING ON HIGHLY LEVERAGED ACHIEVEMENTS AT WORK - DON'T GET SO BUSY DOING YOUR WORK THAT YOU CAN'T DO YOUR JOB

Achievement Nudge #34

Why We Wear Pants

Why do we wear pants? I'll tell you the story, including a nudge to be careful about decisions you make today. Be they good or bad, the results of your decisions today will get embedded into your future. Pants prove the point.

First some history.

The Japanese Kimono, Roman robes and the traditional kilt (also worn by some early Americans); all were not conducive to riding a horse. In "hindsight" (an appropriate word in this situation) it's obvious. But the wearing of these garments persisted until a fashion shift occurred.

Pants, or trousers, were the natural evolution of garments worn as the riding of a horse became more the mainstream way to get around, fight battles and travel. There was some resistance though, particularly in Rome. Some of the more affluent and well-known people continued to try and wear robes. They claimed the reason for not wearing pants to be, "I'm afraid people will laugh at me," a reason that often occurs when there is change on the horizon.

Nevertheless, trousers caught on and became the garment of choice for more than just horse riding. Indeed, today, just walk down the street and see how many men especially, and women too, are wearing pants - and they're not riding horses!

Why we wear pants today came from a decision that had to do with riding a horse. The decision started as an individual decision, continued on to a societal decision, then became the norm.

This process (and its results) is just like what happens when we make decisions. Here's an example...

Look at your closet. Does it have a "norm" in terms of where you hang certain garments? When did you make that decision? Do you think about that decision today, or reevaluate it? Do you test it, determine its validity value, efficacy, or usability? Nope! I bet not. At some point in time, you made a decision, for reasons that may have been forgotten, and the decision stuck!

The analogy of your "closet-decision-making-process" and how it came to be that we wear pants, is a prophecy of what will happen in your future. You make a decision about something and the results of that decision become more durable than the situation that caused it.

The nudge? Think beyond the here and now to the future when you are making significant decisions. Business choices, personal adjustments, relationship decisions, even choosing to rearrange or reorganize people or things - all can have a durable aspect.

Obviously the flip side of this "be careful" nudge is true too. Look for leveraging decisions. Your choice can be durable and extremely beneficial if you make it with the future in mind and manage its ripple effect.

ACHIEVE A BETTER FUTURE BY BEING CAREFUL ABOUT YOUR DECISIONS TODAY

Achievement Nudge

Achievement Nudge #35

When it Matters

We all have the ability to "kick it up a notch," but will we? Often, not until it really matters.

In the movie, Apollo 13, astronauts were stuck in space, completely dependent on their ground crew to figure out how to fix a fatal accident so they could come home. At a critical part in the story, a man poured a pile of parts on the table and said to the engineers, "That's what we have to work with. Figure out how to fix the problem so we can bring them home."

No complaints, no wishing they had something else to work with, no arguments, no distractions – just pure focus. They took into account the limitations and opportunities, then did what none of them had ever done before. Their brains achieved the impossible.

"Sully" Sullenberger, a pilot with US Airways, made a split second decision and successfully landed his crippled plane in the Hudson River, saving all passengers on board. Had he ever done that before? No! He was presented with a problem, considered the limitations and opportunities, and landed the plane in the river.

He didn't complain, didn't wish for something different, didn't argue with reality, didn't get distracted – he just had pure focus. Like the Apollo 13 engineers, his brain did the impossible.

How does a person's brain work like this? Is it possible for all of us? Yes! Most definitely, YES!

Neuroscientists have conducted enough research to prove that our minds are plastic. Not literally (well…except in a few people I know). "Plastic" means the ability to bend, be reshaped, be re-molded, to change – sometimes dramatically. In certain situations, our brains can work in different ways than they ever have before. "***Plasticity" is the mental methodology to reach unbelievable potential.*** And this plasticity is available to all of us until the day we die. It never goes away.

The two illustrations above are examples of plasticity; the brain achieving something amazing and different than ever before. It's remarkable how our brain has the ability to reshape current reality and limitations into something amazing.

But these examples, as dramatic as they are, are no different than when Joann made soup yesterday.

Ok, ok… I know that Joann making soup isn't *exactly* the same as saving hundreds of lives by landing a plane in the river. But the difference in scope and outcome is just that…the difference in scope and outcome. HOW her brain did it is the exact same process.

The soup was delicious and different than anything she had ever done before. She went to the fridge and the cupboard, considered her limitations and opportunities, then created a scrumptious meal. No complaints, no wishing she had different ingredients, no arguments with reality, and she didn't get distracted. Just pure focus. In terms of brain processing, *HER* brain did the "impossible" too.

Scientists say a key factor necessary to engage plasticity is motivation.

> *If it doesn't matter to YOU, it won't matter TO DO.*

They say that a lack of belief, distractions, even boredom can prevent brain plasticity. So focus on what matters to you. Find your heart's desire.

Don't let the plasticity of your brain be nothing more than a plastic jug. Believe in the power and the plasticity of your mental powers to reshape the recourses available and achieve what matters to you.

Use plasticity, with its magical, powerful potential, to help you do the "impossible" too.

It works when you're saving lives, and it works when you're making soup.

ACHIEVE THE IMPOSSIBLE – IF IT MATTERS

Achievement Nudge

 Achievement Nudge #36

The Aikido Approach

There is a technique I created for people attacked by unwanted thoughts or behavior. It worked nicely because I borrowed it from the martial art of Aikido. I'll teach you how to use the move.

Have you ever said, "I shouldn't do (fill-in-the-blank), but I just can't stop"? I've heard it many times. People complain about doing something or thinking something, as if they were forced to do it. They live as victims, stuck in the prison cell of habit. But I found a way to help them.

In the early 80's I had a counseling practice in Napa Valley. During one session, I heard the "…but I can't stop" phrase from one of my patients and an insight fired in my brain. It was based on a premise coupled with the martial art of Aikido.

The premise was this: No one has the right or ability to take away our power of choice, SO at some level, every thought or behavior is a choice.

The Aikido principle I thought of was this: Aikido is the act of becoming one with the universe and reconciling everything into harmony. This is accomplished by becoming one with the attacker's energy and force, then turning it into reconciliation and harmony.

From these insights I gave the following instruction to my patient. When he said, "I shouldn't keep criticizing my wife, but I can't stop," I said, "Then don't stop. Instead, CHOOSE to criticize your wife." He looked shocked. From my perspective, he looked awake!

I explained to him, "You've been trying to resist the force of criticism for some time and it hasn't worked. Yet, at some level, you are choosing to criticize. Let's bring that choice into your conscious mind and own it."

After I fully explained the concept he understood and began to practice my request with immediate results. As soon as he became aware of being critical, I instructed him to become one with that behavior and consciously say, "I CHOOSE to be critical." Then the magic happened. Since he didn't WANT to be critical, he was repulsed by his behavior and choice…and made a new one.

Aikido has been around and proven to work physically since 1942. I was pleased that my "mental Aikido move" worked well too. And it worked with ANY negative attacker. It worked when attacked with unwanted behavior like procrastination. It worked when attacked with persistent negative thinking. It worked when attacked with bad habits like smoking. This mental Aikido was powerful stuff.

I taught people to own their behavior and thoughts by saying, "I

CHOOSE to procrastinate" when they were late on something, "I CHOOSE to think negatively," when barraged with ugly thoughts, "I CHOOSE to smoke" when lighting up. It worked like magic.

Just like in Aikido, becoming one with the attacking energy, allowed the opportunity to divert it or eliminate it. In the process, people learned they weren't victims. They could use choice to re-direct the negative, attacking energy into positive, peaceful reconciliation.

As I watched how the technique worked, I realized that sometimes we are not stuck in our unwanted behavior or thoughts – we are stuck in the belief that we don't have a choice in the matter.

CHOOSING to own what we are doing, thinking, or saying, vaporizes that lie and illuminates this truth: "I DO have the power of choice – even if I'm not making very good ones!"

(By the way; if you choose to keep doing your negative stuff, like criticizing your wife, tell her not to blame me. It's YOUR choice!)

ACHIEVE FREEDOM FROM ATTACK BY USING A MENTAL AIKIDO MOVE

Achievement Nudge

 Achievement Nudge #37

Ten Foot Ceilings

This nudge gives a whole new way to think about "raising the roof." Look around you before you read it, this nudge is going to change your perspective on your surroundings.

Neuroarchitects are scientists who are focused on understanding how your surroundings affect how you think. They have come to understand that they can actually shape how your brain works, by shaping your physical environment. And if *they* can do it, so can you.

A University of Minnesota research study, led by Joan Meyers-Levy, found that a two-foot difference in the height of a ceiling has a subtle, but profound effect on how people approach a problem or consider a new product.

In each test, a ten-foot ceiling caused the people in the study to have more abstract thinking with their thoughts being freer in nature. An eight-foot ceiling consistently caused people to focus on more details or specifics.

It was a subtle yet profound difference, and one that the research subjects didn't even notice or acknowledge. The higher ceiling sparked the places in the brain that created loftier ideas and thoughts. The lower ceiling activated the areas of the brain that produce more constrained or confined thoughts.

Other research went beyond the height of a ceiling to prove that other aspects of our surroundings, such as colors or organization of items, affect our thinking and behavior too.

Many designers of our physical space already intuitively craft an environment that primes our brain functions. A space with warm colors, cozy furniture and a fireplace will invoke a whole different type of brain processing than a corner office in a high-rise building with lots of windows overlooking the city. Snuggling with your honey on a date-night would work well in the first setting, not so much in the second.

What can we learn from this, and how does this learning nudge us?

The first learning is to become conscious of the space you are in and notice whether it is conducive to the work or brain function you are doing. When I do my writing, I sit in a much more expansive space than in my office. Ideas and concepts flow more freely and are much more creative than when I'm sitting at my desk.

What is your space like? Disorganized clutter around you might make you inefficient. Being in a small space such as a cubicle might help your mind confine itself to detail and focus, but limit your ability to think outside the box. Opening or closing the drapes on the windows of your home might affect your ability to think beyond the moment or

Ten Foot Ceilings

be trapped in what's going on right now. You can get a clue about how your surroundings are affecting you by looking at the outcomes of your work within the space you're considering, and paying attention to how you feel within it.

A second bit of learning is to simply own the fact that we are not stuck. Our bodies move. We can go to a different space that is more conducive to how we need to think. And if that's not possible, changing how that space looks and feels typically is possible.

If it is necessary to work in a cubicle, select pictures to pin to the cubicle wall that are congruent with how you want your mind to work. In your home, pay attention to what hangs on the walls, your choice of colors, how the furniture is arranged. I rearranged our living room furniture into a more intimate setting one day and every visitor thereafter commented on how cozy our living room was.

The key here is to become aware of your surroundings, then use your power of choice to create the type of environment you want. To not be conscious of your space perpetuates your past with whatever positive (or negative) outcomes you have been experiencing.

This whole concept makes for some interesting mental exploration. "Telecommuters" work on the telephone. Do "dimwits" work in the dark and "brilliant" people work in a bright place? Do "close-minded" people work in a small space or "absent-minded" people work in an empty space? (I've got to shut down this computer and get out of this open space…my mind is getting WAY too expansive!) Do spendthrifts work in a bank or adorable people work in a…(STOP it Bill, just STOP it!!!)

ACHIEVE A DIFFERENCE IN HOW YOUR MIND WORKS BY CHANGING YOUR ENVIRONMENT

 Achievement Nudge #38

Polymodal Sequence System

I invented a phrase. I know it's unique because I Googled it with quotes (which searches for the exact phase), and what came up was, *"no results found."* So, nowhere in the world will you find this phrase. And if you use it you're going to sound extremely intelligent.

First let me tell you about the situation the phrase describes. Everything you experience is the result of a multitude of differing elements that affect each other and work together in a sequential, systematic way to bring about a certain result. A shorter way to say it is this, everything you experience is because of what came before. I'll explain.

Let's say you want to run by the grocery store on your way to work and pick up some rotisserie chickens for the company picnic. The chickens are the main part of the meal. You've been delegated that task by Cindy, the girl you want to impress.

When you get to the store, there are no chickens – at all. What you don't know is Charles, who cooks the chickens and normally leaves for work at 4:30 a.m. had car trouble. He had to take the bus to work but the next bus didn't come by until 5:00a.m. He arrived late – for the 6th time and got fired. Peter, his replacement, put the chickens in the rotisserie but they weren't going to be done until mid-morning.

Result? No chickens for you. Delegated task failed. Cindy won't speak to you. You never get a date with her. She marries Todd. They buy your dream house and live the life you wanted to live.

You, my friend, are a victim of a ***"polymodal sequence system"***…and that's the phrase I invented. What does it mean?

Definition: ***Poly*** = many; ***Modal*** = various elements, phases, situations; ***Sequence*** = occurrences or things that happen in prescribed order; ***System*** = elements that work together to produce an outcome. ***Polymodal-sequence-system.***

Let it roll around on your tongue for awhile. Notice how easy and fun it is to say. Then use it with a bit of confidence and watch the person you are talking to be impressed.

If your husband comes home from work and complains about all the things that caused him to get home late. Say, "Wow, Honey. You were a victim of a polymodal sequence system."

While listening to your boss explain how sales are down, speak up with your brilliant observation, "Sir, I think we are products of a polymodal sequence system."

Now here's how you can have power over a polymodal sequence system. Do this: Change ANY element ("mode") in a given system and the outcome will change. Even a small change in a relatively trivial part of the system will change the outcome of the polymodal sequence system.

It's a scientific fact. Since everything is connected to everything else in a polymodal sequence system, changing any part of the system changes the entire system - AND the outcome of that system.

Look at your life in the context of a polymodal sequence system. If you experience the same outcome over and over, it is undoubtedly because of a polymodal sequence system. If it's a positive outcome, leave it alone. If it's a negative outcome, change some aspect of the system and you'll get a different outcome.

If Charles had just made a short phone call to Peter to come in early and start the rotisserie, you'd be married to Cindy today.

ACHIEVE CONTROL OVER YOUR LIFE AND THE ILLUSION OF BRILLIANCE BY USING A PHRASE THAT EXPLAINS WHAT REALLY CAUSES THE OUTCOMES OF LIFE

Achievement Nudge

Achievement Nudge #39

Patience From Perspective

Joann has wanted me to write about patience for a long time since, apparently, I am a patient man. But here's the deal – I don't think it's about patience, it's about perspective.

I believe that people who seem to be patient people are simply people who know how to think differently than other people. Every "patient" person I've met lives by a few basic philosophies. I do too. Here are four of them.

1. If it's over – it's over.

Someone backed into our car. Five seconds before, we had a whole bumper, five seconds later, we didn't. EVERY ounce of energy, EVERY second of time spent thinking about life five seconds ago is wasted. I can't change that it happened so I accept that it did, then ask myself, "What's next?" And THAT'S what I think about. No complaints. No re-living the past. No focusing on "what should have happened." Just, "What do I do next?" Because, if it's over – it's over!

2. If you can't do anything about it, don't.

What would you think if you overheard a group of friends in a lengthy argument about what color the sky SHOULD be? Ridiculous, right? Yet, there are so many things in life that people spend energy on. Things they worry about, think about, talk about; yet they have no authority, responsibility or even the *ability* to do anything about those things.

When something comes up for me, I ask myself, "Do I have the responsibility or authority to do anything about this?" If the answer is "no" then I don't think about it. I certainly won't waste any time or energy on it. I believe, if you can't do anything about it, don't!

3. *If you're on the trail you've chosen, stay on it – no matter what comes.*

If you're on a direction you've chosen, stay on it until, or unless, you choose a different direction. On the trails in our life, things can get irritating, angering, distracting, disappointing, or fearful; and often we let those things stop us from walking the trail.

But every trail is going to have unexpected twists and turns, beautiful wayside distractions, or logs to crawl over. Even the environment, or the weather that surrounds you can change – but NONE of those things change which trail you're walking. They are just things you experience while walking your trail.

To waste time and energy focusing on the things that make the trail hard, can keep you from using your time and energy to WALK the trail. If you're on the trail you've chosen, stay on it – no matter what comes

- that is, until or unless you choose to change your trail. You always have that option.

4. If it's a 50/50 chance for two potential outcomes, choose the better 50.

There are so many things we just don't know, like the outcome of an issue or the reason why we are in a given situation. At best it's 50/50. 50% chance of a positive outcome and 50% chance of a negative one.

Now, I find most people choose to believe in the 50% negative possibility over the positive one, then they spend their time and energy there. I don't.

If there's a choice as to what I believe in, a choice of what MAY happen, or what MIGHT have been the reason for what has happened – I choose the better 50. Why not? Nobody says you have to choose the negative one. If you do, YOU are the only person that is hurt by it – and that just doesn't make sense.

Joann thinks all of this makes me a patient man. I don't think it's about BEING patient, I think it's more about how I think – and more specifically, it's about *how I CHOOSE to think.*

Of course, there is another possibility. It's called "denial." But I'm choosing the "better 50!"

ACHIEVE PATIENCE BY CHOOSING YOUR PERSPECTIVE

 Achievement Nudge #40

Wi-Fi

Are you holding on to outdated or useless labels? So is the rest of the world. But sometimes what WE hold on to about our SELVES can be quite damaging.

What does "Wi-Fi" mean? It means absolutely nothing. That's right… nothing. It has become *associated* with something, but by itself – it means nothing. It's like "apple" – it has become associated with a computer but doesn't mean "computer." Let me tell you the story.

If you Google Wi-Fi, you will find "reliable" dictionaries who say it means "Wireless Fidelity" but that definition came from a tag line that was used over 10 years ago that said, "Wi-Fi – the Standard for Wireless Fidelity". But the tag line was dropped rather quickly even though the content hung around as a hand-me-down, socially-perpetuated label. Here is the real story.

In 1999 a few global industry leaders allied together in a non-profit organization with the goal to create a single set of world-wide standards for wireless local area networking (WLAN). They called themselves the "Wireless Ethernet Compatibility Alliance (WECA)." A mouthful in just the name. But there was *even more* "gobble-de gook" *(Now THERE is a technical term)*.

The standards they created were called "IEEE 802.11". Can you tell they must have been technical nerds? What a catchy title – IEEE 802.11. If you Google THAT, you will get an accurate definition: "…a set of standards for implementing wireless local area network (WLAN) in the 2.4, 3.2 and 5 GHZ frequency bands." But this was just too much technical mumbo jumbo for our daily use.

Those techy nerds were smart enough to know they needed another title for the standards than "IEEE 802.11" so they hired Interbrand to come up with a name. This is the company who created some naming strategies for IBM, and named Prozak, Celebrex, the Mitsubishi Eclipse and more.

Interbrand came up with a number of interesting options, but the one that took and stuck was "Wi-Fi;" sort of a play on "Hi-Fi," but it was never intended to mean that or be anything other than a catchy name that was ASSOCIATED with "IEEE 802.11 – the World-Wide Standards for Wireless Local Area Networking."

So, the label was created and we perpetuate the label as if it means something. But in reality, it is a label that is ASSOCIATED with something, yet MEANS nothing. *(Starting to get the point of this nudge?)*

There are experts who insist it means something. There are dictionaries who swear by the "wireless fidelity" definition. There are people who don't believe and can't accept the historical origination of the truth over the perpetuated myth of the lie!!

Ok, I'm getting a bit worked up. But I'm worked up and get angry when I see people become victims of the same kind of process when it comes to perpetuating "lie-labels" about THEMSELVES! Labels that have become *associated* with the individual, but are not really true in their meaning.

It's like these labels: "You'll never amount to anything; You're always late; You can't be depended on; You're not going to make it…" These are labels that probably had a shaky or faulty origin. Yet we perpetuate them, believe them, live by them, are limited by them – we even define ourselves by them! ARRRRGGGGHHH!!!!! Stop it!

This nudge is to look your labels in the eye. Ask if they are true. If they are, do something about them. If not, on your behalf I stand with you and slay any myth of any hand-me-down label that may be associated with you, yet doesn't mean anything at all.

This ends today! Anything that causes you anxiety, fear, sadness, or limitation, disavow it. Let it go. Don't use misguided labels just because they were used before or are simply convenient. Instead, create a new label for yourself. One that is based on TRUTH!

ACHIEVE MORE CONTROL AND FREEDOM BY CHOOSING YOUR LABELS

Achievement Nudge

Achievement Nudge #41

How Happy Are You?

The problem with answering the question, "How happy are you with life right now?" is that your feelings about the question can't be trusted.

When researchers asked two questions of some college students in Germany in the following manner, they got no correlation between the answers.

How happy are you these days?

How many dates did you have last month?

But when the questions were reversed with another group of students, where the dating question was asked first, there was a huge correlation between the two questions. Students who had more dates rated life much happier than those who didn't.

Another research study had participants come to the facility to fill out a questionnaire on happiness and well-being. Each person was asked to go make a photocopy of the questionnaire before filling it out. Half of the participants found a dime on the photocopier planted there by the researchers.

This minor stroke of good fortune caused a clear and decisive difference in the responses to the questionnaire. The participants who found the dime rated life's happiness and well-being higher than those who didn't.

There are many other studies that confirm the same thing. Our view on how well things are going, how happy our life is, how highly we rate our well-being…all are initially evaluated based on our recent experience. How we feel about recent experiences directly influences how we feel about life.

If you want to truly know how happy you are about life, don't go by how you feel. Instead, consciously look at a bigger sample of your life. Consider your entire life (or at least the last large chunk of it – last month, or last year), and let that influence and infect your perspective…which will also affect your feelings. THEN answer the question, "How happy am I in life?" I call it the "Recent Experience Influence."

This "Recent Experience Influence" dynamic is true of anything we evaluate: a friend, our car, our job, our boss, our life, our spouse, our…. you name it. How you evaluate whatever you are looking at and how you feel about it is going to be almost completely determined by the recent interactions with it. 99% of your experience with it will be nuked into oblivion by your subconscious response that favors only remembering what has recently happened.

The nudge is this: Get conscious about the whole "it" (whatever "it" is that you are thinking about - life, job, spouse...), then answer any question in your mind about, "How's IT going?"

ACHIEVE GREATER HAPPINESS BY THE EXPERIENCES OF A BIGGER REALITY OVER YOUR RECENT REALITY OF EXPERIENCES

Achievement Nudge

 Achievement Nudge #42

Keeping Up With the Joneses

Are there are some things in life you can hardly stand not having. Or do you find you want something just because someone else has it? If so, you might have a monkey on your back that you're not even aware of.

Frans de Waal, a primatologist at Emory University taught two monkeys to hand him a rock. When they did they were rewarded with a slice of cucumber, and they liked that! The monkeys were happy and performed nicely. That is, until he changed the reward.

At one point, when the two monkeys handed him the rock, he gave one a slice of cucumber and the other a grape. Now, these monkeys liked grapes just as much as they did cucumbers. But when one monkey got a grape, he went berserk. He began shrieking, baring his teeth, thrashing in his cage and pounding on the table showing anger.

What happened? Scientists call it a "supernormal stimulus," that's what happened. We know this kind of stimulus as "keeping up with the Joneses." The monkey became upset NOT because it didn't like the grape, but because it didn't get what the other monkey got.

A "supernormal stimulus" is when a normal stimulus, which is satisfied with a normal response, becomes amplified into a stimulus that ONLY a CERTAIN response can satisfy. One of the most common ways a normal stimulus gets promoted to a supernormal stimulus is when we compare what we have to what others have. A choice between a cucumber and a grape for the monkey in the research wouldn't have caused the "berserk response." It was the anxiety, fear and anger of being slighted that did.

Recent studies in neuroscience have confirmed this emotional response, even in humans. A supernormal stimulus causes a normal desire to expand from a *psychological* temptation to include a *physiological* one. In other words, we FEEL the power of what we want (and the stress of not having it) more than just the mental desire to have it. Our response is visceral, emotional, and physically demonstrative. There is also an increased amount of stress associated with the desire created by a supernormal stimulus.

To "want" a car in response to the stimulus of needing transportation is one thing. To want a SPECIFIC car because THEY have one adds a layer of anxiety, urgency and stress that goes beyond the normal stimulus, and that can be quite harmful.

The media doesn't help either. Our global access to information has increased our awareness of what others have, and injected more supernormal stimulus into our lives than ever before.

Look at the commercials. There isn't a lone person enjoying that "treat" – it is always a message that everyone else has it, or that ALL "successful, happy, sexy, popular people have this product – you should have it too!"

So…the next time you want that "something," are driven to get that "something," or you start acting like the monkey who didn't get the grape just because you didn't get that something – step back and check out *why you want it.* You just might find yourself wrestling with a supernormal stimulus. And maybe it's time to get THAT monkey off your back!

ACHIEVE GREATER PEACE AND LESS ANXIETY BY NOT "KEEPING UP WITH THE JONESES"

Achievement Nudge

Last Words on the Titanic

I was reading about the Titanic and was moved by a certain fact I hadn't learned before. It resulted in this Achievement Nudge.

In a Time Magazine book about disasters I read the section about the sinking of the Titanic. One small paragraph jumped out and absorbed my attention. I couldn't stop thinking about it and felt the emotion in the mental movie it created in my mind.

There is a brief report from second Officer Charles H. Lightoler who was manning a collapsible lifeboat. As the Titanic was beginning to take her final plunge over two miles to the bottom of the sea, he heard what he said would haunt him the rest of his life.

As he pulled away from the sinking ship he could hear husbands and wives, brothers and sisters, parents and children crying out to each other, "I love you."

I found it interesting that the last words heard were not fearful screams, they weren't curse words, they weren't even cries for help. It seems people accepted the inevitable and expressed the most important thoughts on their mind - words of love to those who were loved.

I compared that story with the many, MANY stories we've heard over the years from spouses and children (even adult children), how they wish they could hear more words of love from those closest to them. And we've heard countless times from employees who wish they were given more recognition and appreciation for the work they do.

So the nudge is this: Don't wait until the ship is sinking and there is not much time left. Look around you and notice those whom you love or appreciate. Then say the words. Relationships are deepened in all fronts and at all levels when you do this.

When I thought about NOT doing this? It truly gave me a sinking feeling.

ACHIEVE A DEEPER RELATIONSHIP BY SAYING THE WORDS BEFORE THEY ARE NECESSARY

Achievement Nudge #44

Psychology of Giving

It truly is more blessed to give than receive. Science proves it. In this nudge you learn how to give the right gift. And when you do, it increases the value of it– to both you and the receiver of the gift.

A group of psychologists from UC Santa Barbara studied gift-giving and found that our brains perceive "generosity" as a "high-return, cooperative strategy". In fact, they found that our brains like giving gifts even more than receiving them. It seems that we humans are wired for generosity even though, at first glance, it goes against traditional economic principles.

The psychologists concocted an elaborate study to determine a person's willingness to give, as well as what happens in our brains when we do. They created a scenario where a participant received a tangible monetary benefit, then was given a choice to keep it or donate some or all of it to a variety of charities. In all cases, the participants opted to give, and to do so generously, even giving anonymously much of the time.

When looking at the brain's response to giving, the results of the study were interesting and surprising. When the participants gave gifts, their brains showed the same neural activity that is activated when receiving a reward. A set of neural pathways were triggered as if the giver received a gift too.

Even more surprisingly, there were two additional benefits that registered in the brain's activity when they gave generously. The "reward center" activity registered MORE when giving generously; AND generosity activated an additional aspect of our brain functioning – that of social connection.

It seems that our brains are wired to give, and to do so generously. But the study revealed even *more* interesting results.

The study went beyond analyzing the giving of a gift to look at the thought process behind the giving. Here, they found some surprising results.

Researchers found that when giving a person something they asked for, say from a list or a known request, that the "reward benefits" are activated in the brain. *But* these benefits were *limited* compared to another type of giving – empathetic, thoughtful, giving.

When you make a thought and time investment in the giving process, it dramatically increases the benefits of the giving, both for you AND the receiver.

First, our "reward neural pathways" are more greatly activated. Second, the recipient is likely to be more appreciative. Third, a surprising outcome showed that generosity, that is both unexpected and spontaneous, is one of the top three predictors of a successful marriage (the other two being sexual intimacy and commitment). Fourth, generous giving makes us feel better about ourselves, we feel happier and we see the world as an overall better place.

Wow...What benefits from giving!!

But what does "generous giving" mean? It became clear that it does not have to do with the type or amount of giving. Generous giving meant taking the time to empathetically get into the mind of the recipient; to thoughtfully choose what would be most meaningful and valuable to that person. "Generous" had to do with "generously giving of your time and attention to choose the right gift." It had to do with the ***process of giving*** more than the gift itself.

And the gift can be a tangible one...OR NOT. Quality time with an aging loved one can be a much more valuable gift than flowers or a book. An unexpected phone call you make to a friend or a loved one to "catch up" can have a positive effect much longer than a "normal" Christmas or birthday gift. A mocha taken to a friend at work can brighten an entire day.

The key to the fantastic benefits of gift giving, for you and the receiver of the gift, lies in the thought behind the giving even more than the gift itself. The research shows your brain is wired to give generously, as defined above, and this increases the value of the gift, even making a gift that is slightly off the mark "spot on" because of the thoughtfulness behind it.

I suppose the little drummer boy had it right when giving his gift to the baby in the manger. A newborn baby misses the heartbeat of a mother and can actually be soothed by light, rhythmic "drumming" that matches the speed of a heartbeat. A silly gift by economic standards; but deeply intuitive, but the little drummer boy showed himself to be empathetic and centuries ahead of his time in the knowledge of what makes a gift valuable. Pa rum pa pum pum!

ACHIEVE HAPPINESS WITH THE RIGHT GIFT

Achievement Nudge #45

Can Money Buy Happiness?

Can money buy you what you really want...like happiness? Here's the truth…

You've heard it said, and possibly have said it yourself, "Money can't buy happiness." And, like me, you might have spoken the words that often go along with that saying, "Yeah…but I'd sure like to give it a try."

The phrase, "Money can't buy happiness," is credited to Jean Jacques Rousseau who was an influential philosopher of the 18th century enlightenment. His original writing said this, "Money buys everything, except morality and citizens," and has since shown up in varying ways such as, "Money can't buy everything," "Money can't buy friends," Money can't buy love," and the popular, "Money can't buy happiness."

But, really…honestly…can't more money buy me just a little more happiness, a bit more peace? Won't winning the lottery relieve my stress and buy me some joy? I'm not sure a wealthy philosopher who lived in the 1700's knows MY situation. He probably didn't even have to pay rent. Maybe money couldn't buy *him* happiness, but I think it would me.

But the research supports the 18th century philosopher. First, notice this. Studies have proven that when we are really honest with ourselves, most people don't really want a LOT of money, they just want more than they have.

If a person makes $1,500.00 a month, they think, "If I could just make $2,000.00 a month I'd be so much better off. The $3,200.00/month person wants $3,800.00/month…and on it goes.

Research showed that people don't really think they will ever become rich so they don't long for that. But they do believe, "If I could make just a bit extra, it would relieve the stress and give me more happiness."

However…there is a problem.

When a person does make a make a bit more money, the lifestyle expands to spend that extra money, and the person is right back where they started – wishing for "just a bit more." What's worse…as they are spending the extra, they really aren't buying a new state of happiness, they're typically just buying more things, more conveniences, more toys.

Now, *that* research focused on those who want or need more money. What about those who already have a lot of it? After all, they're the only ones who would ***REALLY*** know the answer to the question about money buying happiness, right?

I hope this doesn't burst any fantasy bubbles, but money doesn't buy happiness for rich people, either. Rich people confirm that a lot of money can make things easier but it certainly can't buy happiness.

More than once, I have heard a wealthy person speak of instantly trading places with anyone else when faced with the loss of a loved one or child in the hospital with a life-threatening situation. Money is worthless in those moments.

A few years ago, I was talking a with wealthy friend who was having problems with his wife. The problems were torturing him. And even though he had twice as much money as he needed to live the rest of his life, and I was having financial difficulties at the moment, he told me this, "I would trade your financial problems for my relationship difficulties in a heart beat!"

When the economy is tough, you've lost your job, or you're just not making as much money as you need or want...remember this: The lack of money hasn't taken away your happiness, it's taken away your attention as to what makes you happy.

Ask yourself, "What makes me the happiest?" I don't think you'll find the answer in your wallet.

ACHIEVE GREATER HAPPINESS BY ENJOYING WHAT ALREADY MAKES YOU HAPPY, RATHER THAN TRYING TO BUY HAPPINESS

 Achievement Nudge #46

The Bat and Ball Problem

There is a money question that's been around for a long time. See if you can get it right. And in the solving of the problem I'll give you a gift.

A bat and ball cost $1.10. If the bat costs $1.00 more than the ball, how much does the ball cost? The most common and intuitive answer is 10 cents. But if you answered that, you are wrong!

I'll explain – and believe me, it took me some noodling to understand this. Let's do some backwards reasoning. If the ball costs 10 cents and the bat costs $1.00 more than the ball, then the bat would cost $1.10, or at least that's how most people reason it out. Did you too?

But, that can't be right because if you add up the bat at $1.10 and the ball at .10, it makes a total of $1.20 – too much. The correct answer is that the ball costs .05 and the bat costs 1.05, a dollar more than the ball.

The "10 cents" answer is what psychologists call "system 1 thinking." It's that first intuitive, gut response that can serve us well many times when evaluating quality, value, danger or maybe even direction. It does not serve us well when a problem has to be figured out.

Achievement Nudge

Something more complex, like diagnosing an illness, needs more thorough, "system 2 thinking," which takes into account all important factors before making a calculated decision.

So, that's the first lesson in this nudge; use "system 1 thinking" for things that need to be judged for quality and value. Use "system 2 thinking" for problem solving.

But that's not really what I wanted this nudge to be about. That's just the set-up to the following question. If, like most people, your answer was "10 cents," what went on inside of you when you were told, "You are wrong!"? THAT response is where the more meaningful learning is in this nudge.

The conclusion of 10 cents makes such logical sense that it cannot be wrong. What happened inside of you when I told you that you were wrong, when you *knew* you were right?

Did you accept that you were wrong? Did you fight it or get angry? Did you objectively return to the problem and try to figure it out? Replay your reaction to the "you are wrong" statement.

That reaction is a clue to your default response to disagreement, criticism, or judgment. And the REAL key question is, "Did you take it personally?" If your reaction was in any way tied to your sense of worth, value, intelligence or the need to defend self; it may suggest a poor or tentative self-esteem. You may be one who is performing on life's stage, waiting for the audience to determine your worth and value by deciding whether you are right or wrong, good or bad. The audience's evaluation determines your worth, your value.

A healthy response is to take the input, look at the issue and figure out the problem or difference in perspective. In reality, YOU are NOT wrong (in the sense of "you" having an identity of "wrongness"). Instead, you came up with a wrong answer. It's the classic and important distinction between saying, "I am a failure," compared to the healthier perspective, "I failed at…."

The gift in this nudge is the opportunity to learn a bit more about you and your self-esteem by determining whether your reaction was healthy and "issue based" (what are the facts here…), or the less healthy "self-worth based" perspective (I must defend myself).

And here is another way you can observe this distinction. You'll probably tell someone else about this bat and ball problem. When they are wrong, notice your response, which will be another clue about your self-esteem. Do you speak to them in an educative, supportive, "explaining the issue" way? Or do you take the more "self-inflating" stance and say, "You are WRONG, Succa! Na, na, na, na, na, naaaaaa!"

ACHIEVE SELF UNDERSTANDING THROUGH AWARENESS OF YOUR RESPONSES

Achievement Nudge

 Achievement Nudge #47

Expressions of Love

Expressions of love that become predictable aren't expressions anymore – they're expectations!

I read some research about love; why love dies, how it exists in the first place, and how expressions of love affect another person. The study showed that predictable expressions of love don't work so well. It's the random acts of love (yes, like the bumper sticker…) that have the most powerful impact.

I saw the truth in this research as I thought about it. I took it a step further in my mental musings and realized this: predictable expressions actually shift the "ownership" of that expression.

It's like the boss who had his secretary send flowers to his wife every Friday at 3:00 p.m. At first they were welcomed. The very smell of the roses created a sense of intimacy and warmth. That is, until a few Friday's went by. This predictable expression of love shifted, both in what it was and who "owned" it.

At first, when the flowers arrived, the woman would think of them as "his gift". After some time, it shifted to "his obligation". And after more time went by, the roses became "my flowers".

Another illustration is a Christmas bonus. At first, the employee says, "Thank you for **YOUR** gift." After a few years it becomes, "Where is **MY** Christmas bonus." And if the company CAN'T give a Christmas bonus, there is a tremendous amount of complaining and criticism. A bit strange if people remembered that it was a GIFT.

When you become predictable in the giving of a gift, you actually give away the "ownership" of it. You now have changed it into an obligation for you and an expectation of "what is mine" to the other person. It's true of all gifts – even expressions of love.

Now, a ritual, also something predictable, is different. Every morning I get tea for Joann. It's a ritual. The morning-kiss, the annual birthday gift, the anniversary dinner – all are consistent, predictable, expected and come from a relationship of love. So, what makes an expected ritual wanted, but an expected expression not so much?

The famous psychologist Carl Jung says that rituals in cultures, religion, relationships are necessary for bonding. They provide stability, security and a sense of connectedness. Every relationship needs rituals for this reason.

But it also needs random expressions of love. The random, novel, creative acts of love demonstrate that you have given thought to the expression, and the person receiving it is special. When you remember an anniversary with its tradition or ritual, it also tells the other person they are special. It says, "I remember the history of our bond and want to perpetuate it."

In a relationship, one of the worst things you can do is get repetitive and predictable in your expressions of love, OR forget a ritual. This nudge is to move you to create rituals and remember them. It is also to nudge you into shaking it up a bit when giving expressions of love.

I know random, novel, creative expressions of love work. One beautiful day after a snow storm, I walked outside to stand in front of the window where Joann was working. I had my snow boots on, my snow gloves, a cowboy hat…and not much else to keep the cold away. Though I couldn't stay in the cold too long, I held up an "I Love You" sign until she looked, laughed and saw my words of love.

She still remembers this scene, even though it happened 15 years ago (at the time of this writing). Oh…and in case you're wondering…I kept that freezing moment as ONE, random, expression of love, NOT a ritual!

(By the way, you can't use the snow boot scene idea – it's taken!!)

ACHIEVE HEARTFELT EXPRESSIONS OF LOVE BY BEING UNPREDICTABLE

Achievement Nudge

Achievement Nudge #48

Stop Promoting

This nudge might cause you to demote a few people – maybe even fire them. Not in the traditional sense, however. It's a bit strange. I'll explain.

Imagine a strange, ***make-believe world*** where a person in a business promotes someone to a position ABOVE them. Follow me here…

Jane wants to know how she's doing in her business and whether she's liked. To find out, she promotes Peter to a rank above her, then asks Peter to evaluate her. Jane doesn't like what Peter says, so she promotes Ann. She then asks Ann what she thinks. Ann conducts an evaluation of Jane and agrees with Peter. Now Jane is devastated.

Jane's feelings of peace and well-being, her happiness and confidence, her ability to be positive and achieve goals is strongly affected by the evaluations she receives in her business. Since she feels horrible about the evaluations Peter and Ann have given her, she promotes another person, Sam, and asks him to conduct an evaluation of her. Thankfully, Sam gives a glowing report about her which makes Jane feel great… temporarily…but she can't fully trust Sam's evaluation because of Peter and Jane's evaluation.

What does Jane do? Keep promoting people until she hears enough of what she is wanting to hear? It's her business, after all. She can do whatever she wants with it.

But it's not long before she has hoards of people who have been promoted to a rank with authority over her, who give evaluations of her, and who affect her positively or negatively with those evaluations. These evaluations go into her ever growing personnel file, and there never seems to be enough to be conclusive.

Strange? Naw… It happens every day. Let's change the make-believe story just a wee bit and you'll see what I mean.

Jane overhears her brother-in-law say some devastating things about her. Without thinking about it, without really exercising choice, Jane *promotes* her brother-in-law to a place in her mind where his words make a difference about how she feels about herself.

Jane doesn't like what she has heard or how she feels based on her brother-in-law's evaluation, so she promotes her sister and asks her what she thinks. Her sister agrees with her brother-in-law. Yuk!! She's devastated.

Forgetting that SHE gave her brother-in-law's words power, that SHE promoted him and her sister to a rank above her to have authority over her feelings…forgetting that SHE has control over her life and can make choices about the INPUT of others; forgetting all of that, she simply keeps promoting others in the business of her life and falls victim to their input.

It happens every day. It happens to most people. It may be happening to you right now. If it is, here's the nudge: STOP promoting people!

Listen to others. Take their input. Determine whether it's valid or not, whether it's opinion or fact, whether it's important to you or not. Make decisions about what you hear. But keep the authority over the business of your life where it belongs – in YOU!

YOU are the CEO of your own business. Tell others to mind their own. STOP promoting them to levels of authority over you – in fact you might even want to fire a few!

ACHIEVE MORE FREEDOM BY NOT PROMOTING OTHERS TO HAVE AUTHORITY OVER YOU

Achievement Nudge

Achievement Nudge #49

Wink

This nudge is about something you know about, but may not know how much you know about it. (Wink)

Putting the word "wink" at the end of a sentence gives a whole different message. With that little word, your mind goes beyond what is written to what is implied. And it's true for all of us. Except for countries that prevent eye contact, the wink is like a smile; it transcends cultural boundaries.

No one knows the exact history of the wink, but it's been around for as long as anyone knows. In the ancient scriptures, it is referred to negatively in Proverbs 10:10, "He that winketh with the eye causeth sorrow"; and also in a positive way in Acts 17:30, "And the times of ignorance God winked at." Indeed, there are many messages that are given with the wink.

A wink can give encouragement to a person who feels nervous or uncomfortable in an awkward situation. It's like a hug across the room. A double wink can indicate you are saying something sneaky or untrue. Even *speaking* the words, "Wink-wink," can give a message that goes beyond the actual words, "The boss wants to have a chat with you… wink-wink."

A wink can be used to flirt. Apply a wink to the end of a simple comment, and it can turn your comment into something suggestive, evoking a smile from the other person, maybe even some blushing and embarrassment. If you say something to a person, then wink at someone else "in the know," it can indicate a secret shared between you and that person. A wink can say, "I'm just joking," or tell the other person you're not really serious.

If you wink, and time it perfectly with a click of your mouth and the pointing of your finger like a gun (sometimes known as a "clink"), it's a cheesy way of putting emphasis on something, or saying, "I agree." A wink can be a signal. A surprise party can begin with a friend winking at others, signaling the start of the "Happy Birthday" song.

The wink has power, even out of context. Try winking at someone today, out of the blue, "just because." Watch their expression change. They may even squirm a bit. Some might even sneak up to you when you are by yourself and ask, "What did you mean by your wink?" Such power. And all you did was briefly close one eye.

The wink has a long history, can say many things, and is used around the world. But do you know what the strangest thing is about the wink? It's that you understand everything I've said. You didn't go to "wink university," nor did anyone sit you down and teach you about all of the subtle messages or nuances, or the importance of impeccable timing when winking. Yet you understand. You know how to give and receive the messages surrounding a wink. You know, but **how** do you know?

I call it "assimilated learning."

There are literally hundreds of thousands of things you have learned without choosing to; and, most of the time, without knowledge of what you've learned or how you have learned it. It is assimilated, buried in your subconscious, then your autopilot takes over so whenever you encounter "it" you know what to do. You know what to feel. You know what to think. All pre-programmed by "assimilated learning," learning you didn't choose.

Do you like that an autopilot governs much of your life, even your winks? If not, don't bother trying to figure out everything that is in your autopilot. Instead, just turn it off.

You do that by living today (and everyday) on purpose. Make a habit of asking yourself, "Why am I doing this?" Challenge your behavior, your attitudes, your thoughts. You may not change a thing you do, but at least YOU will be in control rather than an autopilot programmed by assimilated learning.

Oh…my term, "assimilated learning," is totally and completely unique. It is derived from years of well-funded research conducted in a total of 23 countries, including research conducted on other planets. (Wink!!!)

ACHIEVE A BETTER TODAY BY TURNING OFF YOUR AUTOPILOT

Achievement Nudge

You Can be a Placebo

This nudge is about how you can give someone a good week without them knowing it. I'll show you how to give them a placebo and have it work in a positive way for them.

When a new drug is being developed, it is literally given to some people while others receive something that looks like the real thing – but it's not. It's called a placebo.

In the group of people who receive the placebo, there is a percentage, sometimes a significant percentage, who experience the positive, healing effects of the real drug, even though they are receiving nothing more than a "sugar pill." It's called the "Placebo Effect" and it has become absolutely consistent, legitimate and documented to be real.

The placebo effect shows the power of the mind to heal when there is belief. From headaches to more serious illnesses, people who receive the placebo can still experience positive, healing effects simply because they believe they will. Though this is fantastic, it's not what I want to focus on.

Much study has been done on the power of the mind to create positive responses in the body through belief, but something occurred to me

Achievement Nudge

that nudged this nudge. Certainly the positive placebo effect wouldn't occur without the element of belief, but it also wouldn't occur without someone administering the placebo. The researcher giving the "sugar pill" is critical to the effect.

I believe a psychic, a horoscope; even a fortune cookie can cause a placebo effect. How many times has your spirit been lifted or you've become more wary depending on the words of a fortune cookie. It's the placebo effect.

It became clear to me; the "giver" of the placebo is just as important as the placebo itself. And, since that's true, you or I can be the administrator of a placebo. I realized, the cookie has no power. But if a fortune cookie can cause this effect, so can some encouraging words from you.

It's proven, researchers ***can't*** avoid the placebo effect. You won't be able to either. Scientists can always count on ***some*** people being helped. It's a given. And so it will be for you.

The placebo effect cannot be experienced without the administrator of the placebo; YOU be that person. This nudge is to reach out to as many people as you can and give them words of support; words that are encouraging, words that create a positive outlook. If you do, you can count on positive results!

ACHIEVE THE ABILITY TO HELP SOMEONE THROUGH THE PLACEBO EFFECT

Achievement Nudge

Achievement Nudge #51

Lost Fingers

I wrote a country song, and actually recorded a demo. No one has picked it up yet – but someday...maybe. It's called, *"Get Your Tongue out of My Mouth, I'm Kissing you Goodbye!"*

Recently, Joann inspired another song idea. Maybe it will be the second song on my future, infamous album. The inspiration came when Joann's mom was rubbing Joann's back. To understand the moment, you need to understand the background.

My mother-in-law has gone through many trials in the past few years, not the least of which was the amputation of her lower right leg, her left foot and some of her fingers. Horrible complications from a 14-hour heart surgery put her on life-support for many weeks. Intense pressure from extremely swollen tissue and some blood clots caused the necessity of the amputations.

She was unconscious after surgery for most of a month. During this time the doctors had to amputate her right lower leg, from the knee down, to keep her alive. When she regained consciousness and was coherent again, they told her about the loss of her leg.

The doctors were understandably apprehensive about what her

reaction would be, but I think all of us underestimated her strength. Her response was something I'll never forget, "Just another part of life's journey" she said.

MOM, YOU LOST YOUR LEG!!

Yet, this is how she lived, and lives, life. Mom has had an incredible attitude of taking life as it comes and not getting upset. She makes whatever adjustments that are needed and lives on. She is a wonderful role model of someone who doesn't blame or get caught up living in the past, or looking for the reasons as to why some bad thing happened. She is the embodiment of the phrase that epitomizes this nudge:

"It may not be your fault, but it is your responsibility!"

We can't choose what happens to us. Our bodies may fail us. The car in the other lane may unexpectedly swerve into ours. A criminal may randomly choose us as the victim of their crime. That trusted employee may unexpectedly turn on us. An extremely rare disease may crawl into our bodies while we sleep peacefully at night.

Our very next moment can be night and day different than the one we're in right now. How you respond to that difference reveals how you use your power of choice. We may never understand the reason or the cause of something horrible that happens to us. But we do have choices about *how* we will respond to it; live in blame, be obsessed with trying to figure out why it happened…or take responsibility for our reaction, consider our options, choose how we will be and what we will do, then move on. That's what mom did. That's what mom does.

And because she lives this way, she can laugh. And she can love. And she can enjoy life. Though she has to make adjustments about how she weeds in the back yard, takes a bath or goes to the store, she still does all those things. And she even jokes about her missing parts. She is a joy to be around.

Now, back to the day she was rubbing Joann's back just like she did when Joann was a little girl. It felt good to Joann even though Mom's hand is missing most of her fingers.

Then…(giggle) and then Joann said the words that caused mom to burst into laughter, AND inspired me with the title to another country song. Joann turned to me and said,

"She hasn't lost her touch, even though she lost her fingers!"

The warmth of our laughter still echoes in my mind, and in my heart. It was a symbolic, teaching moment of how to live this unpredictable life. And speaking of unpredictable… "Look out Blake Shelton. Here I come!

ACHIEVE A HAPPIER LIFE BY TAKING RESPONSIBILITY FOR YOUR PART IN IT

Achievement Nudge

Dad Doesn't Retire

This nudge is simple in content, powerful in its point. And DO take it personally.

At 70 years old, my dad wanted to retire and travel… "But maybe not quite yet," he said.

At 75, Dad wanted to retire and travel… "But maybe a few more years could help us financially," he said.

At 78, Dad wanted to retire and travel… "Though it may take longer, I think we should hold out for the perfect buyer," he said.

At 81, Dad wanted to retire and travel… "I still have the strength and energy to travel so maybe it's time to get more aggressive about selling the business," he said.

April 21, Dad's 82nd birthday, he said, "I think it's REALLY time now…I want to retire and travel!"

Dad died in November.

ACHIEVE YOUR DREAM BY ACTING ON IT

# Acknowledgment

I want to thank Diana Maclean Schenone for her inspiration as I wrote this book. Diana's words of encouragement, and her smiley faces in the margin when giving back a manuscript, were continually motivating. I was especially touched when she was moved to tears by certain Nudges.

I also thank her for reading every word in this book, telling me about that were missing, as well as words that were duplicated duplicated.

I thank her, too, for heling me with misspelling, and puntuation, and showing me the places where, commas, were needed, and, not, needed.,;

By the way - Diana didn't read this page before publishing the book. I wanted to surprise her.

Achievement Nudge

www.ingramcontent.com/pod-product-compliance
Lightning Source LLC
Chambersburg PA
CBHW052019290426
44112CB00014B/2304